Italian
Regional Cooking

Italian
Regional Cooking

Tony Schmaeling

CHARTWELL
BOOKS, INC.

Published by
CHARTWELL BOOKS, INC.
A Division of **BOOK SALES, INC.**
110 Enterprise Avenue
Secaucus, New Jersey 07094

Copyright © RPLA Pty Limited 1981

ISBN 0-89009-565-5

Printed and bound in Hong Kong by South China Printing Co.

Contents

Acknowledgements   8
The Cuisine of Joy   9
Lazio   10
Campania   18
Calabria   26
Sicily   38
Basilicata   46
Abruzzi e Molise   54
Apulia   58
Umbria   66
Tuscany   74
Emilia-Romagna   82
The Marches   90
Lombardy   98
Liguria   118
Piedmont and the Valle d'Aosta   126
Venezia   134
Index   151

THE REGIONS OF *ITALY*

1 Piedmont and Valle d'Aosta • *2* Lombardy
3, 4, 5 Venezia • *6* Liguria • *7* Emilia-Romagna
8 Tuscany • *9* The Marches • *10* Umbria
11 Lazio • *12, 13* Abruzzi and Molise • *14* Campania
15 Apulia • *16* Basilicata • *17* Calabria • *18* Sicily

Acknowledgements

My trip to Italy had been arranged at very short notice and I had no detailed itinerary planned. It was entirely due to the great effort, efficiency and willingness to assist of Giuliana Bartelletti at the ENIT office in Rome that my whole visit was organised.

Throughout Italy, I was also generously assisted by officials and guides of local tourist offices, all of whom gave me hospitality and friendly help: Dir. Luca Vespoli (Positano), Dot. Sergi (Reggio Calabria), Enzo Mauro and Vincenzo Santilio (Matera), Dot. Costa (Taranto); Dot. Boninsegni (Florence), Signora Muta and Signorina Covalini (Bologna), Avo. Marcellini and Constanza Rafaelli (Ancona), Giuseppe Pisilli (Como), Dir. Marchisio and Pietro Giordano (Asti); Signora Fabioletti (Alassio), Dot. Boglione (Aosta), Signora Carlotta (Verona), Drs. Winter and Dosser and Signorina Frass (Bolzano), Mietta Shamblin (Trieste), Antonio Sorgo (Muggia), Signora Muffato and Renzo Salvatore (Venice).

I thank Nicola Mazzara Morresi of Ancona for her charming book on the traditional cooking of the Marches.

The whole project was originally initiated by Kevin Weldon, who was at the time Managing Director of Paul Hamlyn. I thank him and Warwick Jacobson, the company's Publishing Manager for their encouragement and technical support.

I'd also like to thank Warren Brash for introducing me to Graham Turnbull of Traveland, whose company sponsored my travels through Europe to collect material for this Viva! Holidays international series of regional cookbooks.

In London I was greatly assisted by Traveland's Manager, Guy Lindsay-Watson and his staff. While in Rome, the Traveland representative, Signor Pagani and his staff helped to solve my problems with the usual Italian enthusiasm.

Back in Sydney, my faithful secretary, Gwen Flanders and her daughter Michelle, persevered with me as they typed their way through innumerable pages of my illegible longhand which contained many unfamiliar Italian names and phrases.

Maureen Campbell of the Italian Tourist Office, gave invaluable assistance in the translation of many Italian recipes given to me by generous chefs and restaurateurs.

My editor, Susan Tomnay, had a hard job putting the whole book together and her dedication is appreciated.

I thank Paul Ring who was my camera assistant during my journey through Italy and who, like me years before, fell in love with this beautiful country.

Throughout my research into the Italian cuisine, and during my travels, Waverley Root's "The Food of Italy" was my great inspiration.

The Cuisine of Joy

The cooking of Italy has been developed over the centuries by a people with an immense love of life.

The huge variety in Italian food stems from the geography of the land and from the backgrounds of all the different people who have lived there.

Added to that are the many external cultural influences that the country has been exposed to in the almost three thousand years of its legendary and recorded history. The Etruscans, Greeks, Romans, Byzantines, Saracens, Africans, even the Chinese have all left their mark.

And in turn, Italy has left her mark. In the 16th Century, Maria and Catherine dei Medici married French kings. They brought with them from Florence their own cooks who exercised culinary skills not known to the French and they introduced the Court to new ingredients, especially vegetables and fruit. This new knowledge became the basis upon which the haute cuisine of France later developed.

To me, Bernard Shaw's saying "no love is more sincere than the love of food" applies more aptly to Italians than to any other people. They are colourful exuberant people who produce food of such enchanting simplicity that it has become one of the most popular and best loved cuisines in the world.

In my travels through 'la bella Italia', the country so attractive and varied and so dear to my heart (and stomach), I have tried to collect a selection of recipes which will best show the regional diversity of the food.

I hope that as well as being used as a cookery book, it will serve as a guide when travelling through Italy. I am certain that the reader, following my path, will derive as much enjoyment as I have had out of exploring the innumerable restaurants, trattorias, wayside inns and simple food stalls all of which exist to serve the best food the country can offer.

Buon appetite.

Lazio

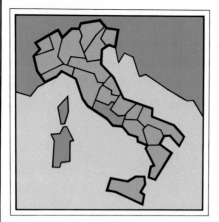

I knew Rome long before I met that city. I was introduced to it at school when history was my favourite subject and later, when I studied the history of architecture at university, it developed into a love affair.

It was a very exciting day in my life when I finally arrived in Rome. I felt so much at home there; I knew the plan of the city and I was able to head straight for sights that were familiar to me, yet never seen before.

*And then of course there was the food: **real** Italian food. I loved the displays of antipasto, vegetables, fruit and cheese near the entrance of the trattorias and tavernas. It all looked so fresh and enticing. And I loved the outdoor eating areas that many of the restaurants have, with their sun umbrellas and waiters in white jackets and aprons.*

Every restaurant in Rome has its own style and atmosphere. There are the simple trattorias with their low ceilings and modest appointments. While at the other end of the scale there's the quiet elegance of fashionable eating places.

Restaurants specialise, and in Rome one can find the cooking of almost every region in Italy. The restaurants that serve purely Roman food do it with pride, and with good reason: the food of Rome is among the best in a country of good food.

Saltimbocca originated in Rome, so did gnocchi alla romana and maccheroni alla ricotta (ricotta is used extensively in Roman cooking). Romans cook lamb in a most delicious way, with olive oil, herbs, garlic and anchovies (abbacchio alla cacciatore) and their spit-roasted suckling pig (porchetta) is the best I've eaten. Romans prepare their vegetables in interesting ways: artichokes with anchovies, spinach with pine nuts and raisins, stuffed tomatoes, peas with onions and prosciutto.

It's unfair when talking about the food of Lazio to speak only of Rome, despite the fact that its cooking dominates the provinces around it.

North of Rome, the town of Montefiascone produces one of the most famous wines of Lazio: Est! Est!! Est!!! There's a wonderful story that goes with its name.

German Cardinal Johann Fugger, who liked his wine, was on his way to Rome to attend the coronation of Emperor Henry V. He sent his steward, Martin, on ahead to find inns which had good wine. His instructions were to write Est (it is) on the inn's door with chalk.

When the Cardinal got to Montefiascone, he found Martin lying in front of a tavern, dead drunk. On the door of the tavern was written Est! Est!! Est!!! The Cardinal missed the coronation.

Frascati wine is also famous and a meal in Rome would be difficult to imagine without a jug of it.

On my first visit to the town of Frascati, I arrived around lunchtime and found striped canvas stalls all along the streets where whole pigs which had been seasoned with herbs, garlic and fresh pepper were being spit-roasted. A chunk of the still warm pork and a bottle of Frascati consumed in a field overlooking the town, is a meal I'll never forget.

The river Tiber winding its way through the historical monuments of Rome.

Stracciatella
'Little Rags'

A Roman speciality, now popular throughout Italy, it is a consommé into which a thin batter of eggs, semolina or flour, grated lemon peel and cheese is poured.

Serves 4

2 eggs
2 tablespoons semolina
½ teaspoon grated lemon peel

2 tablespoons grated Parmesan cheese
5 cups (1.25 litres) chicken consommé
salt

1. In a mixing bowl, beat the eggs and add the semolina, lemon peel and cheese.
2. Add 1 cup of consommé and stir it to smooth cream. Add a little salt.
3. Heat the remaining consommé and when it is nearly boiling, pour in the egg mixture stirring constantly with a fork for 3 to 4 minutes.
4. Bring the soup to the boil and serve immediately; the mixture should have formed into 'little rags'.

Carciofi alla giudia
Artichokes Jewish Style

This recipe comes from Sabatini in Rome. This is an ancient recipe for artichokes as prepared in the Jewish quarter in Rome.

Serves 4

16 small artichokes (in Rome they are known as 'cimaroli')
1 lemon
water

salt
freshly ground pepper
approximately 4 cups (1 litre) olive oil

1. Remove the tough outer leaves of the artichokes and cut off the stems leaving approximately 4 cm (1½ in) of stalk.
2. With a very sharp knife, trim the leaves, shaping each artichoke so that it takes a round shape.
3. As each artichoke is completed, immerse it in a bowl of water into which you have squeezed the juice of the lemon. This will prevent the artichokes from turning black.
4. When all the artichokes are shaped, take them out of the water, drain them well and dry them. Holding the artichoke by the stalk, beat the head of each one against the table so that the leaves flatten out.
5. Sprinkle with salt and pepper.
6. In a deep cast-iron casserole, heat enough oil to completely cover the artichokes. Add the artichokes and cook them for approximately 10 minutes, turning them occasionally so that they are cooked on all sides.
7. Turn up the heat and continue cooking for a further 10 minutes.
8. Remove the artichokes from the oil, drain them and place them on absorbent paper.
9. Arrange them on a serving plate and serve immediately.

Spaghetti alla prestinara, alla carbonara, a cacio e pepe

Three Roman ways of preparing spaghetti. The same recipe may be used for rigatoni (short, thick, ribbed macaroni).

Serves 4

375-500 g (12-16 oz) spaghetti
water
salt

1. Boil the water, add the salt and cook the spaghetti for 4 to 8 minutes depending on the degree of softness desired. Most Italians cook it briefly and serve it 'al dente' (firm).

   (1) **'alla prestinara'**

   A poor man's spaghetti for those who love garlic.
   1 cup (8 fl oz) olive oil (for this dish the best quality should be used)
   3-4 cloves garlic, chopped
   salt
   freshly ground black pepper
   1 cup (4 oz) grated Parmesan cheese

   1. When the spaghetti is cooked, heat the oil in a small saucepan, add the garlic and let it stand for a few minutes without frying it.
   2. Pour the oil over the spaghetti and sprinkle it with the grated cheese.

   (2) **'alla carbonara'**
   125 g (4 oz) prosciutto, smoked ham or bacon, chopped
   2 tablespoons butter
   2 eggs, beaten
   salt
   freshly ground black pepper
   1 cup (4 oz) grated Parmesan cheese

   1. Lightly fry the prosciutto, ham or bacon in the butter.
   2. Add the beaten eggs and briefly cook them until they are just about to turn into scrambled eggs.
   3. Pour the mixture over the cooked spaghetti, season, and stir in half of the Parmesan.
   4. Serve with the remaining cheese sprinkled over it.

   (3) **'a cacio e pepe'**
   salt
   lots of freshly ground black pepper
   1 cup (4 oz) grated pecorino cheese

   1. Add the salt and pepper to the cooked spaghetti.
   2. Sprinkle with the cheese and add some of the hot cooking water from the spaghetti.
   3. Mix well and serve very hot.

Cipolline in agrodolce
Sweet-and-Sour Onions

Serves 4

500 g (1 lb) small pickling-type onions
2 tablespoons olive oil
¼ cup (2 fl oz) white wine vinegar
½ cup (4 fl oz) water
1 tablespoon sugar or 2 tablespoons
  honey

2 cloves
1 bay leaf
1 teaspoon salt

1. Cook the unpeeled onions in water for 10 minutes. When they have cooled, peel them and put them into a clean saucepan with the olive oil. Sauté them lightly for 5 minutes.
2. Add all the remaining ingredients and simmer gently for 30 minutes.
3. Drain and serve hot or cold as part of an antipasto or as a separate vegetable course.

Trippa alla romana
Tripe Roman Style

Serves 6

500 g (1 lb) pre-cooked tripe
2 onions, chopped
2 carrots, chopped
1 stalk celery, chopped
salt
freshly ground black pepper
3 slices bacon, chopped
2 tablespoons olive oil

½ cup (¾ oz) chopped parsley
1 clove garlic, crushed
2-3 slices smoked ham
2 tablespoons tomato paste mixed with
  ½ cup (4 fl oz) water
¾ cup (3 oz) grated Parmesan cheese
6-8 mint leaves, chopped

1. Cut the tripe into thin strips, about 4 cm (1½ in.) long.
2. Place the pieces into a large saucepan and cover with water. Add one of the onions, the carrots, celery and some salt.
3. Simmer for 1 hour, or until almost tender but not completely cooked.
4. Sauté the remaining onion and the bacon in the oil. Add the parsley, garlic, ham and tomato paste mixture and simmer for 5 minutes.
5. Add the tripe, simmer for ½ hour, stirring occasionally. Taste. The tripe should be cooked but not too soft. Season.
6. To serve, sprinkle with Parmesan and mint. It is at its best eaten with fried polenta.

Sabatini, Piazza Santa Maria in Trastevere, Rome.

Sabatini occupies a special place in my mind. It was the first Roman restaurant I ever visited and every time I've been back I've enjoyed really delicious Roman food. I particularly like the way they prepare seafood. Unfortunately it was here also, on the first day of my recent gastronomic tour, that my Hasselblad camera was snatched from the table in front of me. Run by the three Sabatini brothers in two separate restaurants, just around the corner from each other, Sabatini serves excellent spaghetti with clams, charcoal grilled sea bass, spit-roasted lamb, Roman or Jewish-style artichokes and many other local specialities. Both restaurants have character and atmosphere in abundance but when you are sitting in the open in the Piazza Santa Maria in Trastevere, hold on to your belongings.

Above: *A selection of typically Roman antipasti, displayed at Sabatini, clockwise from bottom right: shellfish antipasto; artichokes Jewish style (see p. 12); oysters; artichokes Roman style; mixed seafood antipasto. At rear, prosciutto with a display of fresh fruit.*

Abbacchio arrosto
Roast Lamb with Potatoes

This recipe comes from Sabatini in Rome.

Serves 4

1 tablespoon lard
1 kg (2 lb) leg of milk-fed spring lamb
  (forequarters may be also used)
12 sprigs fresh rosemary

salt
freshly ground pepper
4 potatoes, cut in quarters and
  par-boiled

1. Preheat the oven to 180°C (350°F/Gas 4).
2. Grease an oven dish with lard.
3. With a sharp knife cut pockets all over the meat and fill with sprigs of rosemary. Season with salt and pepper and place it in the dish.
4. Place the potatoes around the meat.
5. Roast the meat for 45 to 60 minutes depending on its thickness.
6. During the roasting turn the potatoes and the meat so that they brown evenly.
7. Serve the lamb cut into pieces or carved into slices garnished with the potatoes.

Coda alla vaccinara
Braised Oxtail, Shepherd Style

Serves 6

2 kg (4 lb) oxtail, cut into pieces
¼ cup (2 fl oz) olive oil
250 g (8 oz) bacon, chopped
½ cup (2½ oz) prosciutto, chopped
2 carrots, chopped
1 onion, chopped
4 cups (1 lb) chopped celery
375 g (12 oz) tomatoes, skinned and
  chopped

1 cup (8 fl oz) dry white wine
2 bay leaves
beef stock
salt
freshly ground black pepper
½ teaspoon cinnamon

1. In a cast-iron casserole, brown the oxtail in half the olive oil.
2. Add the bacon, prosciutto, carrots, onion, and 3 cups of the celery. Fry until golden brown.
3. Add the wine, bay leaves and sufficient beef stock to cover the oxtail. Season, cover and simmer for 3 to 4 hours.
4. Half an hour before the dish is cooked, sauté the remaining celery in the rest of the oil and add to the casserole.
5. Before serving, add the cinnamon and some more ground pepper.

Saltimbocca alla romana
Veal with Ham and Sage

Serves 4

8 thin slices veal scaloppine
8 thin slices prosciutto ham
8 fresh sage leaves
1 tablespoon butter

3 tablespoons olive oil
salt
freshly ground black pepper
1 cup (8 fl oz) dry white wine

1. With a toothpick secure a slice of ham and a sage leaf to each slice of veal.
2. In a frying pan melt the butter and add the oil.
3. Briefly brown the ham side of the veal and then turn it to the meat side, season and add the wine. Simmer for 6 to 10 minutes.
4. When cooked place the meat on a serving platter. Continue to boil the cooking juice to reduce it to half its volume. Season if necessary and serve with the pan juices poured over the meat.

Pangiallo alla romana
Roman Christmas Cake

Makes 1 round cake

⅔ cup (5 oz) sugar
⅔ cup (5½ fl oz) warm water
2¾ cups (11 oz) flour
1 envelope (7 g) active dry yeast
250 g (8 oz) almonds, coarsely chopped
250 g (8 oz) hazelnuts, coarsely chopped

250 g (8 oz) pine nuts
1.5 kg (3 lb) raisins
250 g (8 oz) candied lemon and orange peel, chopped
¼ teaspoon each of cinnamon, cloves, nutmeg, allspice
3 tablespoons oil

1. Over low heat dissolve ½ cup of the sugar in ¼ cup of the water.
2. Dissolve the yeast in 4 tablespoons of water and add it to 2¼ cups of the flour and the sugar syrup in a mixing bowl. Mix well. The dough should have a soft consistency; if necessary add more water.
3. Add the almonds, hazelnuts, pine nuts, raisins, candied peel and spices.
4. On a floured board knead the dough until smooth and elastic.
5. Shape the dough into a ball, place on a buttered baking tray and let stand in a warm place for approximately 12 hours.
6. Preheat the oven to 190°C (375°F/Gas 5).
7. Dissolve the remaining sugar in 1 tablespoon of water, stir in the remaining flour, the oil and some cinnamon. Make into a thick batter and pour it over the dough.
8. Bake in the preheated oven for 45 minutes or until cooked.
9. Cool before serving.

Campania

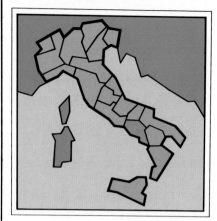

If the Campania, and especially Naples, had no other claim to fame, the pizza would have carried its name around the world.

It is said to be of Roman origin (minus the tomatoes of course).

Today there are countless varieties and every Neapolitan household prides itself on its own version. The basic regional dish is the pizza alla napolitana, made with mozzarella cheese, fresh tomatoes, tomato paste, anchovy fillets and oregano.

The tomato is an indispensable ingredient in most Neapolitan cooking, followed closely by the green pepper.

The cooking of the Campania is simple peasant food. Meat is a luxury but there's plenty of fish and many of Campania's most famous dishes are made from seafood. Fritto di pesce (mixed fried seafood) and zuppa alla marinara (fish chowder) are two that immediately spring to mind.

The Campania produces some well-known cheeses. From the milk of the buffalo, not as plentiful today as in the past, the farmers produce the 'true' mozzarella and provolone cheeses, sometimes also made from cows' milk.

The region is well-known for spaghetti, macaroni and similar dry pastas served al pomidoro (with tomatoes), al sugo (with meat sauce), alle vongole (with clam sauce) and in many other ways.

Only second in fame to the pizza is Neapolitan ice cream, rich in flavour and creamy, filled with the fresh aroma of fruit and berries.

The food of the Campania is generous, hearty and rustic, just like the people.

Fishing boats on beach at Positano.

Zuppa di vongole

Neapolitan Clam Soup

Serves 4

48 clams (pippies, mussels or cockles
  may be used)
2 cups (16 fl oz) dry white wine
1 leek (the white part only), chopped
1 onion, chopped
1 clove garlic, crushed

2 tablespoons olive oil
4 cups (1 litre) fish stock
1 large tomato, peeled and chopped
1 teaspoon fresh chopped marjoram
3-4 leaves of celery, chopped
4 large croûtons, fried in butter

1. Place the clams in a saucepan, pour in the wine and gently cook until the clams open.
2. Drain, save the liquid and remove the shells.
3. Sauté the leek, onion and garlic in the oil, add the liquid from the clams and the fish stock.
4. Stir in the tomato, marjoram and celery leaves.
5. Simmer for 10 minutes, stir in the clams and serve hot, poured over the croûtons.

Zuppa di pesce caprese

Capri Fish Soup

Serves 4-6

3 tablespoons olive oil
2 onions, thinly sliced
3 stalks celery, chopped
2 cloves garlic, crushed
1 teaspoon each fresh marjoram,
  thyme and basil
1 kg (2 lb) tomatoes, peeled and
  chopped
1 teaspoon grated lemon rind

freshly ground black pepper
1 cup (8 fl oz) dry white wine
1 cup (8 fl oz) water
250 g (8 oz) octopus, chopped
1 kg (2 lb) mussels, scrubbed
8 prawns (shrimps), uncooked
12 thick slices fresh tuna, or any fish
  steaks
4-6 slices bread, fried in butter

1. In a saucepan, heat the oil and add the onions, celery and garlic. Sauté for 5 minutes. Add the herbs, tomatoes, lemon rind and black pepper. Cook for a few minutes.
2. Add the wine and simmer, covered, until the tomatoes are reduced to a pulp. Add the water and simmer for a further 3 minutes.
3. Add the octopus and cook on a low flame for 20 to 30 minutes or until it is tender.
4. Add the mussels and cook until the shells open.
5. Add the prawns, cook for 3 to 5 minutes, peel and reserve them.
6. Add the fish, cook for 5 minutes then return the prawns to the pan.
7. Season and serve with slices of fried bread.

Crespolini al formaggio
Cheese and Spinach Pancakes

Serves 4

PANCAKE BATTER:
1 cup (4 oz) flour
1 teaspoon salt
2 eggs
1 tablespoon olive oil
1¼ cups (10 fl oz) milk
olive oil (for frying)
PANCAKE STUFFING:
¼ cup spinach purée
½ cup (4 oz) ricotta cheese (cream or
  cottage cheese)
1 egg
3 chicken livers, chopped and quickly
  fried in butter
salt
freshly ground black pepper
¼ teaspoon nutmeg

CHEESE SAUCE:
2 tablespoons butter
2½ tablespoons flour
1 cup (8 fl oz) hot milk
6 tablespoons grated Parmesan cheese
salt
pepper
mozzarella cheese, one slice for each
  pancake

Pancakes
1. In a bowl, blender or food processor, combine the flour, salt, eggs, 1 tablespoon of oil and the milk. Blend to a smooth and creamy batter. Refrigerate for ½ hour.
2. Put a few drops of oil in a pancake pan and heat.
3. Pour sufficient of the batter into the pan to make a thin pancake. Fry on both sides until golden-brown. Continue making pancakes until you have used all the batter. This amount of batter will make at least 8 pancakes.

Stuffing
1. In a bowl, combine the spinach purée, ricotta, egg and the butter-fried livers. Season and add the nutmeg.

Cheese Sauce
1. Melt the butter in a small saucepan, add the flour and cook for a few minutes without browning.
2. Gradually add the hot milk, stirring constantly, and cook for 5 minutes.
3. Remove the sauce from the heat, stir in the grated cheese and season.

To Assemble the Pancakes
1. Preheat the oven to 200°C (400°F/Gas 6).
2. Place an equal amount of filling on each pancake and roll each like a cannelloni.
3. Place the rolled pancakes, one next to the other, in a buttered oven-proof dish.
4. Pour the sauce over the pancakes and place a slice of mozzarella cheese over each pancake.
5. Put the dish into the preheated oven and cook for 20 to 25 minutes until the top is brown.

Pizza alla napoletana
Neapolitan pizza

From Chez Black in Positano.

Serves 4

DOUGH:
4 cups (1 lb) flour
1 teaspoon salt
1 tablespoon sugar
1½ teaspoons dry yeast
½-¾ cup (4-6 fl oz) lukewarm water

FILLING:
1 kg (2 lb) tomatoes, peeled and
  chopped
⅓ cup (2½ fl oz) olive oil
½ teaspoon salt
1 teaspoon sugar
1 clove garlic, crushed
90 g (3 oz) mozzarella cheese, sliced
2 teaspoons chopped oregano or basil

Dough
1. Place the flour on a board, make a well in the centre and add the salt and sugar. Dissolve the yeast in a little of the water and stir it into the flour, adding enough water to make a soft dough.
2. Beat and pummel the dough until it becomes smooth. Lift the ball of dough and hit it against the board until it is smooth and elastic.
3. Divide the dough into 4 parts, form them into balls and allow them to rise for 2 to 2½ hours.

Filling
1. Preheat the oven to 200°C (400°F/Gas 6).
2. Cook the tomatoes with half the olive oil, the salt, sugar and garlic for 30 minutes.

Preparation of Pizza
1. Roll out the balls of dough into rounds about 6 mm (¼ in) thick and place them on a greased baking tray.
2. Spread the cooked tomatoes over the rounds and place the slices of cheese on top of the tomatoes. Sprinkle with the oregano or basil and pour over the remaining olive oil.
3. Place the baking tray in the preheated oven and bake for about 30 minutes. Serve hot.

Calzone
Turnover Pizza

Serves 6

½ of the dough recipe for pizza
  Napoletana (above)
6 slices prosciutto or smoked, cooked
  ham
6 slices mozzarella or Bel Paese

2 tablespoons olive oil
salt
freshly ground black pepper

1. Preheat the oven to 200°C (400°F/Gas 6).
2. Prepare the dough as described for pizza Napoletana, roll it out very thinly and with a teacup, cut out rounds of dough.
3. On one side of each round lay a piece of ham and a slice of cheese, sprinkle it with oil, salt and pepper.
4. Fold over to form a half-moon shape and press the edges together to enclose the ham and cheese.
5. Grease a baking tray, arrange the calzone on the tray and bake in the preheated oven for 20 to 30 minutes. (The calzone may also be deep-fried in very hot oil.)

Chez Black, Positano

Salvatore Russo, the owner of Chez Black, was so suntanned that the English visitors to Positano nicknamed him 'Black'. This was some 15 years ago but the name stuck. When, in conjunction with Giuliana Bartelletti, I was planning my trip through Italy, I was at first very surprised that she suggested Positano as the place to try a Neapolitan pizza. However, when the chef at Chez Black pulled the pizza out of the oven (right), I knew why. It looked great. The fresh, peeled tomatoes were bright and red and the mozzarella and Parmesan gave off a most tantalizing aroma. The flavour matched the appearance: black, pitted olives gave it pungence while the taste of fresh basil completed the great combination. Positano, from a sleepy fishing village of pre-war years, has developed into a very popular tourist resort. However, it has retained its charm and pretty setting on the slopes of the Amalfi coast. Its seafood is unsurpassed, fresh and expertly prepared.

Above: *spaghetti marinara as prepared at Chez Black.*

Fritto misto

Mixed fry

Serves 4

BATTER (PASTELLA):

3 tablespoons olive oil	12 flowerets cauliflower
salt	2 potatoes, peeled and cut into 1.5 cm
½-¾ cup (4-6 fl oz) lukewarm water	(½ in) slices
1 cup (4 oz) flour	flour
1 egg white	salt
125 g (4 oz) calves' liver	freshly ground black pepper
250 g (8 oz) calves' brains	½ cup (4 fl oz) melted butter mixed
250 g (8 oz) veal fillet	with ¼ cup (2 fl oz) olive oil

1. First make the batter: stir the oil, salt and water into the flour and let it stand in the refrigerator for 2 hours.
2. Just before using, whisk the egg white stiffly and fold it into the batter.
3. Trim and rinse the liver, brains and veal. Cut them into bite-sized pieces.
4. Dip them and the cauliflower and potatoes in flour, then dip them in the batter and fry them over medium heat in the butter-oil mixture for 3 to 5 minutes or until golden-brown.
5. Drain the pieces on absorbent paper, sprinkle with salt and serve immediately.

Note: If you substitute fresh seafood for the meat in this recipe, the dish is called Fritto di pesce.

Spaghetti alla napoletana

Spaghetti with Tomatoes, Cheese and Bacon

Serves 4

1 medium-sized onion, cut in half and sliced	tomatoes, finely chopped
	1 tablespoon tomato purée
1 stalk celery, finely sliced	salt
1 small carrot, finely chopped	freshly ground black pepper
1 clove garlic, crushed	375 g (12 oz) spaghetti
¼ cup (2 fl oz) olive oil	155 g (5 oz) pecorino cheese, grated
2 slices bacon, cut into fine strips	200 g (6½ oz) mozzarella or fresh
⅔ cup (5½ fl oz) dry white wine	ricotta cheese, diced or crumbled
4 ripe fresh tomatoes or canned	1 teaspoon dried oregano

1. Lightly brown the vegetables in the oil together with the bacon.
2. Add the wine and cook until it has almost evaporated.
3. Add the tomatoes, tomato purée, and season it with salt and pepper.
4. Cook this mixture until it is thick, stirring occasionally.
5. Cook the spaghetti in lots of boiling water until cooked but still firm.
6. Drain the spaghetti and add the vegetable mixture and one tablespoon of pecorino.
7. To serve, place the spaghetti into a bowl and sprinkle it with mozzarella or ricotta and oregano. Serve the rest of the pecorino separately.

Costoletta di maiale alla napoletana
Neapolitan Pork Chops

Serves 4

4 pork loin chops
flour
salt
freshly ground black pepper
6 tablespoons olive oil

2 cloves garlic, crushed
2 cups (16 fl oz) tomato purée
125 g (4 oz) mushrooms, chopped
3 green peppers (capsicums), cut into
  strips

1. Trim the fat from the chops, flatten them with the side of a knife, dust them with flour and sprinkle with salt.
2. Heat half the oil and fry the garlic. Add the chops and fry them until brown on both sides. Remove them and keep them hot.
3. Add the tomato purée to the pan juices, season and simmer for 5 minutes. Add the mushrooms and simmer for a further 5 minutes.
4. Return the chops to the pan and simmer for 15 minutes.
5. Sauté the strips of pepper in the remaining oil, season.
6. To serve, arrange the pork chops on the dinner plates, mask them with the sauce and place the cooked pepper strips on top.

Bistecca alla pizzaiola
Neapolitan Steak

Serves 4

4 rump steaks, about 2.5 cm (1 in)
  thick
PIZZAIOLA SAUCE:
10 ripe tomatoes, peeled and chopped
2 tablespoons olive oil
2 cloves garlic, crushed

2 tablespoons chopped parsley
½ teaspoon oregano
1 teaspoon sugar
salt
freshly ground black pepper

1. Combine all the sauce ingredients in a saucepan, bring to the boil and simmer, uncovered for 15 to 20 minutes.
2. Grill the steaks to your liking and serve with the sauce poured over them.

Gelato di fragole alla napoletana
Neapolitan Strawberry Ice Cream

Serves 6

1½ cups (12 fl oz) cream
½ cup (4 oz) caster (powdered) sugar

1½ cups (12 fl oz) thick strawberry
  purée

1. Turn the refrigerator control to the coldest setting at least 1 hour in advance.
2. Whip the cream with the sugar until it is thick.
3. Gently fold in the puréed strawberries.
4. Transfer to empty ice cube trays and freeze for 1 to 2 hours.
5. Tip the frozen mixture into a bowl and break it up with a hand beater.
6. Return the mixture to the trays and freeze for a further 1 to 2 hours.
7. Repeat the beating-up and finally refreeze for 2 to 3 hours before serving.

Calabria

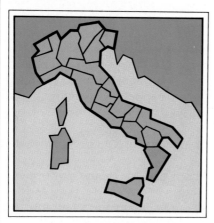

Today, only ruins give an indication of Calabria's illustrious past. As the centre of ancient Magna Grecia, many places still bear Greek names.

Now known as one of the poorer regions of Italy, it is difficult to imagine that in those far off days it was renowned for its wealth which was, to a great extent, derived from the land. Certainly Calabrese cooking today does not show any signs of the luxuriously excessive style of Sybaris.

Basically it is peasant cooking: its main ingredients are pasta and vegetables. What little meat there is, is reserved for festive occasions.

The coastal towns have the benefit of fish, most particularly tuna and swordfish. They are usually prepared in very simple ways: for example, tuna steaks, brushed with olive oil and lemon juice and sprinkled with parsley, garlic and pepper, are grilled over a wood fire.

But mostly the people eat thick soups made from pasta and vegetables especially eggplant, tomatoes, green peppers and artichokes. These vegetables are also cooked by themselves in various ways, usually stuffed and fried or baked.

In the interior regions, a little game can be found and sometimes this is roasted, cut into small pieces and served with pasta (maccheroni con l'arrosta – macaroni with roast).

The only area with any wealth at all is the region immediately surrounding the city of Reggio Calabria. It is in this area that bergamots are grown. They are a citrus fruit, similar to a large lemon in appearance which are never eaten, but used in the manufacture of eau de Cologne. Reggio Calabria makes millions of dollars every year from the sale of bergamots. They are not grown commercially anywhere else.

Wherever you go in Calabria and whatever food you eat, you can be sure that it will all be heavily peppered and spiced. It is the flavour of the south.

Aerial view of Cozenza in Calabria.

Pancotto
Bread Soup

Serves 6

500 g (1 lb) tomatoes, peeled, seeded
  and roughly chopped
1 cup (8 fl oz) olive oil
4 sprigs parsley, chopped
3 bay leaves
1 clove garlic, crushed

3 stalks celery, chopped
salt
pinch cayenne pepper
8 cups (2 litres) hot water
12 slices bread, toasted
grated Parmesan cheese

1. Fry the tomatoes in the oil, add the parsley, bay leaves, garlic, celery and salt. Sauté for 5 to 10 minutes.
2. Add the cayenne pepper and the water.
3. Pass the soup through a sieve.
4. Break up the toasted bread into chunks and put them into the soup.
5. Serve immediately, sprinkled with Parmesan cheese.

Pizza calabrese
Calabrian Pizza

Serves 6

PIZZA DOUGH:
4 cups (1 lb) flour
1 teaspoon salt
7 g dried yeast or 15 g fresh yeast
½ cup (4 fl oz) lukewarm water
6 tablespoons lard
2 egg yolks (keep some of it for glazing
  the top of the pizza)
TOPPING:
1 kg (2 lb) ripe tomatoes, peeled and

  chopped
½ cup (4 fl oz) olive oil
1 clove garlic, crushed
1 teaspoon basil leaves, chopped
1 cup tinned tuna, drained
¾ cup (4 oz) black olives, pitted and
  halved
4 anchovy fillets, chopped
1 tablespoon capers
freshly ground black pepper

1. Mix the flour and the salt. Dissolve the yeast in the lukewarm water and add to the flour, mixing it to form a soft dough. If necessary add more water. Knead the dough for several minutes, place it in a floured bowl, cover it with a towel and let it stand and rise for 1 to 1½ hours.
2. When it has risen, beat the dough with a wooden spoon and add the lard and the egg yolks. Knead it on a floured board until it is soft and elastic and does not stick to the board.
3. Divide the dough into two parts, the one for the bottom should be twice the size of the one for the top.
4. Roll out the larger piece to line the bottom of a 30 cm (12 in) pie tin leaving an overhang of 1.5 cm (½ in).
5. Preheat the oven to 230°C (450°F/Gas 8).
6. In a saucepan, combine the tomatoes, olive oil, garlic and basil and cook to a thick consistency.
7. Cool the mixture and add the tuna, olives, anchovies, capers and pepper.
8. Pour the sauce on top of the dough in the pie tin.
9. Roll out the second piece of dough to a diameter large enough to cover the pie. Roll the lower edge over the lid.
10. Glaze the lid with a mixture of the remaining egg yolk and a tablespoon of water.
11. Let the pizza rest at room temperature for 20 minutes.
12. Bake in the preheated oven for 25 to 30 minutes or until the top is golden brown. Serve hot.

Maccheroni alla calabrese
Calabrian Macaroni

Serves 6

¾ cup (6 fl oz) olive oil
1 clove garlic, crushed
1 small hot chilli (optional)
1 onion, finely chopped
155 g (5 oz) prosciutto ham, finely
  chopped
1.25 kg (2½ lb) tomatoes, peeled,
  seeded and roughly chopped

salt
pepper
625 g (1¼ lb) macaroni
125 g (4 oz) Caciocavallo (or Cheddar)
  cheese, grated

1. In ½ cup of the oil sauté the garlic and chilli. When the garlic is brown, discard it.
2. Add the onion, and cook until golden brown.
3. Add the ham and cook for a further 5 minutes. Add the tomatoes, season with salt and pepper and cook on a medium heat for 35 to 40 minutes.
4. Cook the macaroni in salted water to the 'al dente' stage.
5. Drain the water, pour the remaining olive oil into the macaroni and mix it well.
6. In an ovenproof dish arrange a layer of macaroni, sprinkle it with grated cheese and pour over some of the sauce. Place a further layer of macaroni, and more cheese sauce in the dish, alternating until all the macaroni cheese and sauce are used up. Finish up with a layer of cheese.
7. Place the dish under a hot grill, brown the cheese and serve while hot.

Maccheroni con vongole o cozze
Macaroni with Clams or Mussels

Serves 4

1 kg (2 lb) clams or mussels
2 cloves garlic
3 tablespoons olive oil

1 red chilli, chopped
345 g (11 oz) macaroni
¼ cup chopped parsley

1. Wash the clams or mussels carefully.
2. Place them in a large heavy-bottomed pan. Cover and heat them, without water, until they open.
3. Keep the liquid from the clams but discard that of the mussels.
4. Remove and discard the shells. Fry the garlic in the oil and when it has coloured lightly, add the chilli. Cook for a few minutes then add the clams and their liquid, or the mussels, and heat through.
5. Separately, in lots of boiling salted water, cook the macaroni until it is 'al dente'.
6. To serve, place the macaroni in a bowl, add the shellfish and sauce and sprinkle with chopped parsley.

Lasagna alla calabrese

Calabrian Lasagna

Serves 6

TOMATO SAUCE:
4 tablespoons olive oil
125 g (4 oz) fresh Italian sausage,
  peeled and chopped
125 g (4 oz) fresh Italian hot sausage,
  peeled and chopped
2 teaspoons fresh basil, chopped
2 cloves garlic, crushed
salt
freshly ground pepper
4 tablespoons tomato paste
4 cups (1 litre) tomato purée

NOODLES:
500 g (1 lb) lasagna noodles
salt
boiling water

FILLING:
2 cups (1 lb) ricotta or cottage cheese,
  crumbled
1½ cups (7 oz) roughly grated
  mozzarella cheese
375 g (12 oz) fresh mushrooms, sliced
4 tablespoons butter
¼ cup (1 oz) grated Parmesan or
  Romano cheese

1. To make the tomato sauce, heat the oil in a saucepan, add the two types of sausage, the basil, garlic, salt and pepper.
2. Sauté for 3 to 5 minutes, then add the tomato paste and tomato purée. Simmer the sauce until it is fairly thick.
3. Boil the lasagna in a large saucepan of salted water a few at a time to prevent sticking. Remove the cooked pieces and plunge them into cold water.
4. Preheat the oven to 200°C (400°F/Gas 6).
5. Oil a baking dish, place a layer of lasagna in the dish, then a layer of ricotta mixed with the mozzarella and then a layer of mushrooms which have been previously sautéed in the butter. Over the mushrooms pour a layer of tomato sauce.
6. Repeat the above and finish up with a layer of tomato sauce. Sprinkle the top with grated cheese and bake in the preheated oven for 30 minutes. Serve very hot.

Spaghetti ammollicato

Spaghetti with Anchovy Sauce and Breadcrumbs

Serves 6

1¼ cups (10 fl oz) olive oil
10 anchovy fillets, cut into small
  pieces

1¼ cups (5 oz) fine dry breadcrumbs
pinch of cayenne pepper
625 g (1¼ lb) spaghetti

1. Use half the olive oil and fry the anchovies; during the cooking time use the back of a fork to mash the anchovy fillets into a paste.
2. Separately, in the rest of the oil, fry the breadcrumbs until crisp and golden.
3. Sprinkle them with the cayenne pepper.
4. Separately, boil the spaghetti in salted water until soft but firm.
5. Drain the spaghetti and mix in the anchovy sauce.
6. Serve it hot with the breadcrumbs sprinkled on top.

Conti, Reggio Calabria

It is unthinkable to go to Reggio Calabria and not to try the famous and delicious swordfish of the Strait of Messina. The season for it is April to July, and while at Conti in May I had the opportunity of eating it at its best, moistened with local olive oil, lightly sprinkled with salt, grilled for three minutes on each side and served with chopped oregano, parsley, freshly ground pepper and a little garlic. As anywhere in the south, great emphasis is placed on baked or fried vegetables and the 'maccarruni 'i casa au ragu', which is local dialect for home-made macaroni with sauce, is better than any macaroni I have ever tasted before. Conti serves a wide variety of Calabrese dishes and rightly deserves the reputation as the best restaurant in Reggio Calabria.

Above: *A selection of dishes as prepared at Conti. From left: casserole of peppers (see p.34); mixed seafood antipasto; stuffed tomatoes (see p.36).*

Spaghetti al sugo

Spaghetti with Tomato and Vegetable Sauce

Serves 4

500 g (1 lb) spaghetti
salt
SAUCE:
½ cup (4 fl oz) olive oil
2 cloves garlic, sliced
½ medium-sized eggplant (aubergine),
   peeled and diced
6 ripe tomatoes, peeled and cut in
   pieces

2 green peppers (capsicums)
1 tablespoon fresh basil, chopped
1 tablespoon capers
4 anchovy fillets, cut into small pieces
12 black olives, halved and pitted
salt
freshly ground black pepper

1. Boil the spaghetti in plenty of salted water for about 10 minutes or until tender.
2. To prepare the sauce, heat the oil in a frying pan, add the garlic and fry until brown; remove it from the oil. Add the eggplant and the tomatoes and simmer for 30 minutes.
3. Place the peppers under a grill and turn them on all sides until the skin starts to blister and can be easily peeled off.
4. Seed the peppers and slice them, add them to the pan together with the basil, capers, anchovy fillets, olives, pepper and salt. Cover the saucepan and simmer for 10 minutes.
5. To serve, mix the sauce into the cooked spaghetti.

Melanzane al funghetto

Sauté of Eggplant

The term 'al funghetto' applies to certain vegetables fried in small pieces with their skins on.

Serves 4

3-4 unpeeled eggplants (aubergines),
   diced
salt

½ cup (4 fl oz) olive oil
2 cloves garlic, chopped
4 tablespoons parsley, chopped

1. Cut the unpeeled eggplant into small dice. Put them into a bowl and sprinkle them with salt. Leave them to drain for 1 hour.
2. Heat the oil in a large frying pan and gently fry the eggplant for about 15 minutes.
3. About 5 minutes before they have finished cooking, add the garlic and just before serving, the parsley.
4. If the eggplant has not absorbed all the oil, drain it before serving.
5. The eggplant thus prepared can be served as a vegetable with meat or chicken dishes or by itself as a separate vegetable.

Melanzane ripiene
Stuffed Eggplants

Serves 4

4 large egg plants (aubergines)
125 g (4 oz) white bread, without
  crusts
1 cup (8 fl oz) milk
8 anchovy fillets, chopped
12 black olives, seeded and chopped
¼ cup parsley, chopped

2 cloves garlic, crushed
1 tablespoon capers
1 tablespoon fresh marjoram, chopped
salt
freshly ground black pepper
¼ cup (2 fl oz) olive oil

1. Preheat the oven to 180°C (350°F/Gas 4).
2. Cut the eggplants in half and scoop out most of the flesh from each, leaving a thin layer attached to the skin.
3. Soak the bread in the milk, then squeeze it dry in your hands.
4. Chop the eggplant flesh and mix it with the remaining ingredients except the oil.
5. Taste before adding salt, as the anchovy may make the mixture sufficiently salty.
6. Put the stuffing back into the eggplants and arrange them on a baking tray.
7. Pour a little oil over each eggplant, cover the dish and cook in the oven for approximately 30 to 40 minutes.

Carciofi gallico marina
Artichokes, Calabrian Style

Serves 4

½ cup finely chopped parsley
4 fresh mint leaves, finely chopped
1 clove garlic, finely chopped
salt

freshly ground pepper
2-4 cups (16-32 fl oz) water
8 artichokes
1-2 cups (8-16 fl oz) water

1. Preheat the oven to 160°C (325°F/Gas 3).
2. Place the parsley, mint leaves and garlic in a cup with salt, pepper and two to three tablespoons of oil.
3. Trim off the external tough leaves of the artichokes and leave approximately 4 cm (1½ in) of stalk.
4. With a spoon open up the leaves and in between them place some of the above mixture. Press the leaves together and arrange the artichokes in an oven dish with high sides.
5. Add salt, pepper and the water and oil, making sure that the artichokes are completely covered. If necessary add more water and oil.
6. Cover the casserole and place them in the preheated oven for approximately 30 minutes.
7. When cooked, drain the artichokes and serve. They may also be served cold as an hors-d'oeuvre.

Peperoni alla calabrese

Casserole of Peppers (Capsicums)

From Fata Morgana in Reggio Calabria.
This dish may be served as a cold hors-d'oeuvre or hot as a vegetable with a main course.

Serves 4

4 large peppers (capsicums)
4 tablespoons olive oil
3 large onions, sliced
315 g (10 oz) tomatoes, cut into four
    and seeded

2 tablespoons white wine vinegar
salt
60 g (2 oz) green olives, stoned and
    sliced

1. Cut the peppers into four and remove the seeds.
2. In a frying pan, heat the oil and brown the onions, then add the tomatoes and the peppers.
3. When all the vegetables have browned, sprinkle with the vinegar. Add salt and after cooking it for about 10 minutes, add the olives.
4. Mix well and when the peppers are cooked, but not too soft, transfer to a serving plate.

Insalata di cavolfiore

Cauliflower Salad

Serves 4-6

1 medium-sized cauliflower
salted water
juice ½ lemon
salt
freshly ground black pepper

⅓ cup (2½ fl oz) olive oil
8 anchovy fillets, finely chopped
2 tablespoons capers
3 sprigs parsley, chopped
12-16 black olives

1. Boil the cauliflower in the salted water until it is tender but firm, depending on the size, approximately 5 to 8 minutes.
2. Drain and rinse with cold water.
3. Combine the lemon juice, salt and pepper with olive oil and stir together to make a dressing.
4. Break the cauliflower into flowerets and arrange them on a serving dish. Pour the dressing over them and sprinkle with the anchovy fillets, capers and parsley.
5. Arrange the olives around the cauliflower and serve.

Fata Morgana, Gallico Marina, Reggio Calabria
The Fata Morgana is typical of the many modest local trattorias which serve some of the best regional food throughout the whole country. Unassuming in appearance, with very little atmosphere except for its beach setting, the Fata Morgana specialises in seafood and is proud of its great variety of vegetable antipasti: peperoni fritti, melanzane arosto, olive schiacciate and antipasto del mare, which combines seafood and vegetables. The Strait of Messina, which the restaurant overlooks, is famous for its swordfish. At Fata Morgana the chef serves it very simply: grilled and sprinkled with olive oil and lemon juice. It's a great delicacy, not to be missed.

Above: *A selection of vegetable antipasti as prepared at Fata Morgana. Clockwise from bottom right: Russian salad; olive schiacciate; roasted peppers.*

Pomodori ripieni di cannolicchi

Tomatoes Stuffed with Cannolicchi Pasta

This recipe comes from Conti in Reggio Calabria.
This dish may be served either hot or cold as a first course or as a vegetable with the main course.

Serves 4

8 large tomatoes
salt
freshly ground pepper
2 tablespoons olive oil

1 cup (5 oz) small macaroni-type pasta
2 tablespoons chopped parsley
6 fresh mint leaves, finely chopped

1. Preheat oven to 160°C (325°F/Gas 3).
2. Cut the tops off the tomatoes and reserve them.
3. With a spoon, carefully empty the inside of each tomato taking care not to break up the pulp. Place the tomatoes upside down on a rack and let them stand for half an hour to drain.
4. Season the inside with salt and pepper and place the tomatoes on a lightly-oiled baking dish.
5. Separately boil the pasta in some lightly salted water. When cooked 'al dente', drain and place the pasta in a mixing bowl. Season, and add oil, parsley, mint and the tomato pulp. Mix well together.
6. Fill the tomatoes and cover them with their lids.
7. Place the tomatoes on an oiled baking dish and put them into the preheated oven for half an hour.

Insalata Conti

Salad of Beans and Tuna

From Conti in Reggio Calabria.

Serves 6

3 medium-sized potatoes, boiled and sliced
½ cup (3 oz) dried white beans (first soaked then boiled until tender)
½ cup (2½ oz) black olives, pitted and cut in quarters
1 clove garlic, crushed
2 tablespoons parsley, chopped
2 teaspoons fresh basil, chopped

¾ cup (6 fl oz) olive oil
4 anchovy fillets, chopped
juice 1 lemon
salt
freshly ground black pepper
½ tablespoon capers
125 g (4 oz) tuna, diced and drained of its oil
185 g (6 oz) crab meat, cooked

1. In a salad bowl, gently combine the potatoes, beans, olives, garlic, parsley and basil.
2. Heat the olive oil and add the anchovy fillets, mashing them with the back of a fork until they are well blended. Add the lemon juice and season, then add the capers.
3. Pour three-quarters of this dressing over the salad and toss it thoroughly.
4. In the centre of the salad make a well and into it place the tuna. Around it arrange the crab meat, sprinkle the rest of the dressing over the tuna and crab meat and serve.

Triglie alla calabrese
Calabrian Mullet

Serves 4

⅔ cup (5½ fl oz) olive oil
4 mullet, cleaned and washed
salt

freshly ground black pepper
juice ½ lemon
1 tablespoon fresh oregano, chopped

1. Heat three-quarters of the oil in a large frying pan and place the fish in a single layer.
2. Sprinkle with salt, pepper, lemon juice and oregano. If necessary add the remaining olive oil.
3. Cook over high heat for 6 to 8 minutes on each side. Serve immediately.

Asticciola alla calabrese
Calabrian Stuffed Beef Rolls

Serves 4

12 thin slices fillet of beef
12 slices mozzarella cheese
24 thin slices Italian-type sausage
8 small pieces stale bread

8 bay leaves
½ cup (4 fl oz) olive oil
salt
freshly ground black pepper

1. Flatten the slices of meat with a rolling pin and in the centre of each, place a slice of cheese and on top of that, place 2 slices of sausage.
2. Roll up the slices and put them on skewers, 3 beef rolls on each, with a piece of bread and a bay leaf in between each roll.
3. Dip the skewers in the oil, season and place them under a hot grill for 6 to 8 minutes, turning them several times to brown them on all sides.

Fichi ripieni
Stuffed Figs

Serves 4

12 ripe fresh figs
¼ cup (1 oz) chopped mixed nuts
1 tablespoon drinking chocolate
1 tablespoon mixed candied fruit, chopped

1 tablespoon honey
2 tablespoons icing (confectioners') sugar

1. Cut the figs in half vertically and from each piece scoop out one teaspoonful of the flesh.
2. In a bowl mix it with the rest of the ingredients, except the icing sugar.
3. Place this mixture back into the figs. Put the two halves together and serve them dusted with the icing sugar.

Sicily

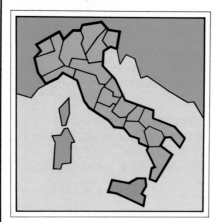

I always used to think of cassata when I thought of Sicily: that rich, delicious sponge cake with layers of strongly flavoured ricotta, the whole covered with a thick coating of chocolate icing.

But this is a very limited view: surrounded by the warm waters of three seas and with all parts of the island within a short distance of the coast, seafood plays a very important part in Sicilian cooking. Tuna and swordfish are the most prized fish – tuna in Palermo and swordfish in Messina. But smaller fish are eaten all over the island too, battered and fried, baked with olive oil, onions, tomatoes and capers, stewed and served with pasta. Mussels and sardines are plentiful too.

Sicilians have a way with vegetables: their salads are delicious and no one can prepare eggplant like a Sicilian. Caponata is one of the most famous eggplant dishes. Its basic ingredients are eggplant, peppers, tomatoes, onions and celery. Depending upon where it is cooked, the dish may also include anchovies, olives, artichokes, octopus or hard-boiled eggs. Meat is not plentiful, but when it does appear on a menu it's usually cooked in delicious and unusual ways like braciola, which is roast pork stuffed with pine nuts, raisins and almond paste.

There's a huge variety of dried pasta in the Sicilian cuisine, much of it served with sauces made from various combinations of tomatoes, eggplant, olives, capers, anchovies, garlic and parsley. Like most southern cooking, Sicilian food is strong in flavour and spicy. Many of its dishes show Greek, Arab and even African influence.

My second misconception about Sicily was the way I imagined it would look. I had visions of a sun-parched landscape, with the grey trunks and dull green leaves of olive groves. I saw it in May and the country was a lush green, with meadows full of spring flowers and fields of young crops.

Picturesque town at the foothills of Mt. Etna.

Pasta con le sarde alla palermitana

Pasta with sardines

This can be prepared with any small white-fleshed fish.

Serves 4

20 g (¾ oz) raisins
200 g (6½ oz) fennel bulbs
1 onion, chopped
4 tablespoons olive oil
8 anchovy fillets, chopped
1 clove garlic, crushed
20 g (¾ oz) pine nuts
¼ teaspoon saffron

¼ cup (2 fl oz) fish stock
400 g (13 oz) fresh sardines, scaled,
    cleaned and dried
½ cup (2 oz) flour
400 g (13 oz) macaroni
oil for frying
salt

1. Preheat oven to 180°C (350°F/Gas 4).
2. Soak the raisins in warm water for 15 minutes.
3. Simmer the fennel for 10 minutes in lightly salted water. Save the water.
4. Drain the fennel and chop into small pieces.
5. Lightly sauté the onion in 2 tablespoons of the oil for 5 minutes, add the fennel and
   cook for a further 5 minutes.
6. Add the anchovies, garlic, raisins, pine nuts and saffron. Cook for 5 minutes more,
   add the stock and continue cooking over low heat for 15 minutes.
7. Dust the sardines with flour and fry them in the remaining oil. Drain them on kitchen
   paper towels and sprinkle with salt.
8. Boil the water in which the fennel was cooked and cook the macaroni until done to
   your liking.
9. Drain and mix half of the sauce into the macaroni.
10. Oil the inside of a casserole or baking dish and on the bottom put a layer of the pasta.
    Cover it with half the sardines. Spread a layer of sauce over them. Top it with the
    remaining pasta and then use up the rest of the sardines. Finally cover them with the
    remaining sauce.
11. Bake it in the preheated oven for 10 minutes. Serve it hot directly out of the dish.

Crocchetti di riso alla palermitana

Palermo Rice Croquettes

Serves 4

1 cup (6 oz) rice
2 cups (16 fl oz) veal stock or milk
salt
2 tablespoons chopped parsley
1 cup (5 oz) cooked meat or poultry,
    finely chopped
¼ teaspoon cayenne pepper

½ cup (2 oz) grated Parmesan cheese
1 egg, well beaten
½ cup (2 oz) flour
1 egg, beaten with one tablespoon of
    water
½ cup (2 oz) fine dry breadcrumbs
oil for deep frying

1. Cook the rice in the stock or the milk and add some salt. The rice should be cooked
   when the liquid is absorbed.
2. Remove the rice from the heat and stir in the parsley, meat, cayenne pepper,
   Parmesan and egg.
3. Cool the mixture and form into croquettes, dip them in flour and let them dry for one
   hour.
4. Dip the croquettes in the egg and water mixture and then coat them with
   breadcrumbs.
5. Heat some oil to 200°C (400°F) and fry them until they are golden brown. Drain on
   absorbent paper and serve accompanied by tomato sauce.

Melanzane alla siciliana

Eggplant with Cheese

From the restaurant 'A Cuccagna in Palermo.

Serves 4

4 eggplants
salt
1 cup (8 fl oz) olive oil
¼ cup (1 oz) flour
2 eggs, lightly beaten

250 g (8 oz) mozzarella cheese, thinly sliced
2 tablespoons finely chopped fresh oregano

1. Preheat oven to 160°C (325°F/Gas 3).
2. Cut the eggplants into slices approximately 6 mm (¼ in) thick. Place them on a large rack or sieve and sprinkle with salt. Leave for 1 to 2 hours until all the liquid has drained off. Rinse them under running water and dry thoroughly.
3. In a large frying pan, heat all but 1 tablespoon of the oil. Dust the eggplant slices with flour, dip them in the egg and fry them, a few at a time, in the oil until golden brown.
4. Drain them and place on absorbent paper.
5. In an oven dish, arrange a layer of eggplant, a layer of sliced mozzarella on top of that, sprinkled with the oregano. Repeat the layers.
6. Sprinkle the top with the remaining olive oil and place the tray in the preheated oven for 10 to 20 minutes.
7. Serve with fresh tomato sauce.

Caponata alla siciliana

Sicilian Ratatouille

A speciality of 'A Cuccagna in Palermo.

Serves 6

1 kg (2 lb) eggplants (aubergines), cut into cubes
salt
500 g (1 lb) onions, sliced
½ cup (4 fl oz) olive oil
500 g (1 lb) tomatoes, peeled, seeded and chopped

2 tablespoons capers, washed
90 g (3 oz) celery stalks, roughly chopped
½ cup (2½ oz) pickled olives, stoned
½ cup (4 fl oz) white wine vinegar
1 tablespoon sugar

1. Arrange the cubed eggplants on a rack or in a sieve. Sprinkle with salt and allow to stand for 1 to 2 hours until the liquid has completely drained off.
2. Sauté the onions in half the oil and when golden brown add the tomatoes, capers, celery and olives.
3. Brown all these ingredients and remove the pan from the heat.
4. Lightly squeeze any remaining liquid from the eggplant and dry the pieces in a cloth.
5. In the remaining oil in a separate pan, fry the eggplant and when brown, drain off the oil and add the eggplant to the above mixture.
6. Add the vinegar and sprinkle with sugar. Mix well and continue cooking over a low heat until most of the liquid has evaporated.
7. Caponata may be served cold as an hors-d'oeuvre or hot as a vegetable with the main course.

Vongole alla siciliana
Sicilian Steamed Clams

Serves 4

3 tablespoons olive oil
2 cloves garlic, crushed
2 tablespoons finely chopped parsley

freshly ground black pepper
48 clams or pippies, scrubbed

1. In a saucepan, heat the olive oil and add the garlic and parsley. Sauté for a few minutes without browning the garlic. Add some pepper.
2. Add the clams or pippies, cover the saucepan and, over a moderate heat, simmer until the clams have opened.
3. Serve the clams in their shells in soup plates with the cooking juice poured over them.

Trance di pesce alla siciliana
Sicilian Fish Steaks

Serves 4

½ cup (4 fl oz) olive oil
4 fish steaks (kingfish, snapper etc.)
1 tablespoon finely chopped parsley
2 cloves garlic, crushed
½ cup (4 fl oz) white wine vinegar
1 kg (2 lb) tomatoes, peeled, seeded and coarsely chopped

salt
freshly ground black pepper
1 kg (2 lb) fresh peas, shelled
4 croûtons, browned in oil

1. In a large frying pan, heat the oil and lightly brown the fish. Add the parsley, garlic and vinegar.
2. Simmer until the vinegar has almost evaporated, add the tomatoes and peas and season to taste. Simmer for a further 10 minutes or until the peas and the fish are tender.
3. To serve, arrange the pieces of the fish on a serving platter and pour the tomato and pea sauce over them. Serve with croûtons.

Tonno alla marinara
Tuna with Olives and Capers

Serves 4

4 slices tuna, about 4 cm (1½ in) thick
4 tablespoons oil
¼ cup (1 oz) dry breadcrumbs
6-8 basil leaves, chopped
12 green or black olives, stoned

3 tablespoons capers
400 g (12½ oz) ripe tomatoes, peeled and chopped
salt
freshly ground black pepper

1. Preheat the oven to 160°C (325°F/Gas 3).
2. In a heavy baking dish, lightly fry the tuna pieces in half of the oil.
3. Sprinkle the tuna with the breadcrumbs and basil leaves.
4. Mix the olives, capers and tomatoes. Season and pour the mixture over the fish.
5. Pour the remaining oil on top and cook in the preheated oven for about 40 minutes.
6. Serve straight from the baking dish.

'A Cuccagna, Palermo

'A Cuccagna means 'abundance' in the local dialect and the first thing one sees upon entering the restaurant is the rich and lavish display of some of its dishes. The meal I ate there was truly Sicilian: caponata, eggplant and artichokes, all 'alla siciliana', macaroni with sardines and involtini. Not to be outdone by their fellow Sicilians along the Strait of Messina, here too they serve a very fine swordfish. The wines of course were also all Sicilian with the inevitable Corvo Rosso accompanying the involtini. I love the rich flavour of Sicilian dishes and 'A Cuccagna showed the local dishes at their best.

Above: *Vegetable antipasti as prepared at 'A Cuccagna. Clockwise from bottom right: eggplant with Parmesan; broad beans; Sicilian ratatouille (see p.40).*

Pollo grillettato alla siciliana

Sicilian Sautéed Chicken

Serves 4

3 tablespoons butter
¼ cup (2 fl oz) olive oil
1 chicken, cut into pieces
250 g (8 oz) very small onions,
   parboiled for 5 minutes in salted
   water

salt
freshly ground black pepper
½ cup (4 fl oz) Marsala wine
2 tomatoes, peeled, seeded and diced
2 sprigs parsley, chopped
½ cup (4 fl oz) chicken stock

1. Heat the butter and the olive oil in a large sauté pan, add the chicken pieces and the onions and brown on all sides. Season with salt and pepper and add the Marsala. Simmer until the wine is reduced by half.
2. Add the tomatoes, parsley and chicken stock.
3. Cover and continue to simmer for 30 to 45 minutes until the chicken is tender. If necessary add more stock during the cooking.
4. To serve, arrange the chicken on a hot serving platter and pour the sauce over.

Filetto alla siciliana

Beef Fillet Sicilian Style

Serves 4

1 tablespoon butter
2 tablespoons bacon, diced
1 onion, sliced
4 slices beef fillet or rump
salt

freshly ground black pepper
1½ tablespoons melted butter
½ cup (4 fl oz) Marsala wine
¼ cup (2 fl oz) water or stock

1. Melt the butter in a frying pan and fry the bacon until it is brown. Add the onion and brown it slightly.
2. With a slotted spoon remove the onion and bacon and keep them warm.
3. Put the slices of meat in the hot butter and fry over a high heat for 2 to 3 minutes on each side. Season with salt and pepper, add the melted butter, Marsala and stock.
4. Lower the heat and simmer the meat for 2 to 3 minutes on each side. Add the bacon and onion and serve.
Note: Dry sherry may be used instead of Marsala.

Zabaione

Serves 4

6 egg yolks
2 whole eggs

8 tablespoons caster (powdered) sugar
1 cup (8 fl oz) Marsala

1. In a bowl, beat the yolks and the whole eggs together with the sugar until they are white and frothy.
2. Stir in the Marsala and pour the mixture into a double boiler.
3. While the water is boiling, whisk the mixture with a hand beater, making sure that it does not get too hot and curdle. As soon as it thickens pour the zabaione into glass dishes and serve immediately.

Cassata alla siciliana
Sicilian Cream Cheese Cake

Serves 6

750 g (1½ lb) ricotta cheese
1 cup (8 oz) sugar
1 teaspoon vanilla essence
2 tablespoons crème de cacao
125 g (4 oz) bitter chocolate, coarsely
  grated

½ cup (3 oz) candied fruit, chopped
  (reserve some for decoration)
1 dozen lady fingers (sponge fingers)
½ cup (4 fl oz) brandy
¼ cup (1½ oz) icing (confectioners')
  sugar

1. Combine the ricotta, sugar, vanilla and crème de cacao.
2. Beat the mixture until it is smooth and fluffy. Add the grated chocolate and the candied fruit and mix well.
3. Line a circular baking dish with waxed paper.
4. Dip the lady fingers in the brandy and arrange them in a fan-shape on the bottom and sides of the baking dish. Be careful not to oversoak the lady fingers or they will fall apart.
5. Put the ricotta mixture into the baking dish, filling it right to the very top. On top of the ricotta arrange another layer of the lady fingers which have been moistened with brandy.
6. Refrigerate for a few hours or overnight.
7. Turn the cassata out of the baking dish on to a plate. If it does not come out easily, immerse the pan in boiling water.
8. To serve, sprinkle the top of the cassata with icing sugar and decorate with candied fruit.

Granita di limone
Lemon Water Ice

Serves 6

½ cup (4 oz) sugar
2½ cups (20 fl oz) water

6-8 lemons (enough to produce 1¼
  cups (10 fl oz) lemon juice)

1. Dissolve the sugar in the water and boil for 5 minutes.
2. Cool the syrup and add the lemon juice.
3. To make the granita, place it in a metal tray and freeze.
4. If you have an electric ice cream machine, churn until the granita sets.

Basilicata

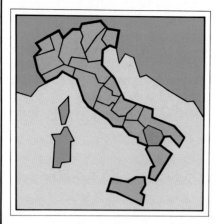

    Until recently few tourists visited Basilicata. New roads, industry and modern methods of farming have helped bring Basilicata into the 20th Century.

    But it is its past that holds the most interest for the tourist. Places like Matera are living museums of continuous human habitation from the Stone Age caves and the dwellings of the early Christians to the Middle Ages and the Renaissance.

    Basilicata is a poor area, mountainous and difficult to cultivate. And its cuisine is basically hearty peasant food. Unlike most other parts of Italy, the people of Basilicata like their food hot and spicy. Ginger is used a great deal and so are hot red pimentos. Prepared meat, probably the only product of Basilicata that is well-known outside the area, often contains both these. The sausages are smoked and aged before being sent to the northern cities, particularly Milan, where they are very popular. And Basilicata's smoked ham is very highly prized throughout Italy. Because Basilicata's coastlines are so short and the cliffs are so steep, salt-water fish plays a very small part in the cuisine of the area. Nevertheless, the fish dishes that do appear on menus are delicious, especially the mixed seafood salads. One of the most famous dishes of the area is arrosto misto, a selection of spit-roasted lamb, flavoursome sausages and lamb intestines wrapped around liver. This is usually accompanied by Aglianico del Vulture, a sturdy full-bodied red wine.

Temple at Metaponto.

Zuppa di cipolle
Onion Soup

Serves 6

750 g (1½ lb) onions, sliced
¼ cup (2 fl oz) olive oil
salt
freshly ground black pepper
6 cups (1.5 litres) beef stock

250 g (8 oz) potatoes, peeled and cut
  into small cubes
6 slices bread, toasted and broken into
  chunks
grated pecorino cheese

1. In a heavy-bottomed saucepan, lightly sauté the onions in the oil. Add salt, pepper, beef stock, and potatoes.
2. Cover and simmer for 45 minutes.
3. Serve it hot with the bread and sprinkled with the cheese.

Sedano al forno
Roasted Celery

Serves 4

2 heads of celery, broken into stalks
  and cut into 7.5 cm (3 in) lengths
juice ½ lemon
salt
6 tablespoons olive oil
1 onion, sliced

4 slices bacon, chopped
pepper
625 g (1¼ lb) tomatoes, peeled, seeded
  and roughly chopped
3 sprigs parsley, chopped

1. Preheat oven to 180°C (350°F/Gas 4).
2. Simmer the celery in water, lemon juice and salt for 15 minutes, drain.
3. In half the oil, sauté the onion and the bacon in a frying pan for approximately 5 minutes.
4. Arrange the celery in an ovenproof dish and pour the onion and bacon over it. Add the tomatoes and the rest of the olive oil. Sprinkle with salt and pepper.
5. Cover the dish and cook it in the preheated oven for approximately 1 hour.
6. Serve it hot, sprinkled with chopped parsley.

Maccheroni con finocchio
Macaroni with Fennel

Serves 6

3 fennel bulbs
salt
juice ½ lemon
750 g (1½ lb) macaroni

¼ cup (2 fl oz) olive oil
freshly ground black pepper
grated pecorino cheese

1. Blanch the fennel in salted water to which the lemon juice has been added, for approximately 15 minutes.
2. Remove the fennel, cool it and cut it into thin strips.
3. In the fennel water, cook the macaroni until tender but still firm.
4. Drain the water.
5. Add the olive oil, the fennel, salt and pepper and serve it sprinkled generously with grated cheese.

Cavatelli e rape alla materana

Cavatelli and Turnips Matera Style

A speciality of Calla, a restaurant in Policoro.

Serves 6

800 g (1 lb 10 oz) turnips, sliced
salt
350 g (11 oz) cavatelli (or orecchiette,
  earshaped-type pasta)
½ cup (4 fl oz) olive oil

1 salted anchovy fillet
½ clove garlic, crushed
½ cup (2 oz) coarse dry breadcrumbs
½ hot red chilli, finely chopped or
  powdered

1. Boil the turnips in salted water for approximately 5 minutes then add the pasta and cook it for approximately 10 minutes, or until the pasta is 'al dente'.
2. In a heavy-bottomed saucepan heat the oil and add the anchovy and garlic. Break up the anchovy with the back of a fork, add the breadcrumbs and the chilli.
3. Drain some of the water from the pasta but leave sufficient to make enough soup for 6 servings. To this add the above mixture and season if necessary.
4. Serve hot in soup bowls.

Filetti di baccalà

Fried Fillets of Salt Cod

Serves 4

750 g (1½ lb) soaked salt cod (if
  soaked cod is not available, soak it
  for 24 hours, changing the water
  every 8 hours)
¾ cup (3 oz) flour
⅔ cup (5 fl oz) water

3 tablespoons olive oil
salt
1 egg white, beaten stiff
1 cup (8 fl oz) olive oil for frying
salt
freshly ground black pepper

1. Skin the cod and cut it into 5 x 15 cm (2 x 6 in) strips.
2. To make the batter, stir together the flour, water, oil, salt and pepper until smooth.
3. Whisk the egg white until it is stiff and fold it into the batter. Let it stand for 2 hours before using it.
4. Dip the pieces of cod in the batter and fry them in hot oil for 4 to 5 minutes until brown and crisp, turning once. Season.

Pollo con peperoni
Chicken with Peppers

Serves 4

5 large green and red peppers
  (capsicums)
1 large onion, sliced
2 tablespoons butter
3 tablespoons olive oil
1.5 kg (3 lb) chicken, cut into pieces

salt and freshly ground black pepper
½ cup (4 fl oz) dry white wine
750 g (1½ lb) tomatoes, skinned and
  chopped
1 cup (8 fl oz) chicken stock
3 tablespoons fresh basil, chopped

1. Place the peppers into boiling water for 1 minute. Drain, peel the skin, remove the seeds and cut the peppers into 2.5 cm (1 in) strips.
2. Sauté the onion in the butter and oil until light brown, add the chicken and brown it on all sides. Season with salt and pepper.
3. Add the wine and cook until it has almost evaporated, then add the tomatoes and stock.
4. Cover and simmer over low heat, stirring occasionally for 45 minutes or until the chicken is tender.
5. Remove the chicken to a preheated serving plate and reduce the pan juices by fast boiling. Pour them over the chicken and serve sprinkled with the basil. If basil is not available, sprinkle with chopped parsley.

Pollo ripieno alla lucana
Basilicata Stuffed Chicken

Serves 4

6 chicken livers, chopped
3 tablespoons olive oil
salt
freshly ground black pepper
2 eggs
4 tablespoons grated Parmesan cheese

1 sprig oregano, chopped
1 sprig rosemary, chopped
1 x 1.5 kg (3 lb) chicken
1 cup (8 fl oz) water
1 cup (8 fl oz) dry red wine

1. Preheat the oven to 190°C (375°F/Gas 5).
2. Lightly sauté the chicken livers in the olive oil, add the salt and pepper.
3. Lightly beat the eggs and add the drained chicken livers, Parmesan, oregano and rosemary and season with salt and pepper.
4. Place this mixture into the cavity of the chicken and, using skewers, secure the opening.
5. Rub the chicken with salt and pepper and moisten it with olive oil.
6. Place the chicken in a baking dish and pour the water and wine into it.
7. Roast the chicken in the preheated oven for approximately 1 hour, basting it from time to time with the water and wine mixture.
8. To serve, cut the chicken into small pieces.
9. Season to taste and serve the chicken masked with the juices as a sauce.

Callà, Policoro

The Ionian Sea supplies the coastal towns of Basilicata with a wide variety of fish and seafood, so that it is not surprising that in the small fishing town of Policoro, Vincenzo Callà serves a delicious insalata di mare, a mixture of baby octopus, mussels, prawns, squid and anchovies in a dressing of chopped parsley and celery, olive oil, lemon juice and vinegar. Callà is also well known for its range of hand-made pasta: fusilli, a type of long, hand-made macaroni; little delicate cavatelli; tagliatelle; gnocchetti di semolino; and delicious cappelletti stuffed with mozzarella cheese, prosciutto and nutmeg. He serves these in a variety of strongly flavoured sauces so typical of the region which enjoys highly flavoured food. Local wines were served but only the Aglianico del Vulture was worth remembering.

Above: *Mixed seafood salad against the background of a hand-painted horse-drawn cart.*

Coniglio alla lucana

Rabbit in Vinegar Sauce

Serves 6

2 rabbits (use saddle and hind legs
  only)
½ cup (4 fl oz) olive oil
2 cloves garlic, crushed
3 sprigs sage, chopped
salt

freshly ground black pepper
1 cup (8 fl oz) white wine vinegar
2 cups (16 fl oz) water
4 anchovy fillets, finely chopped
3 tablespoons capers

1. In a heavy-bottomed casserole, sauté the rabbit together with the garlic, sage, salt and pepper until the meat has browned.
2. Add the vinegar and water to the casserole, cover and simmer for 45 minutes.
3. Add the anchovy fillets and capers, and simmer for a further 15 minutes.
4. Season to taste and serve the rabbit with the sauce in which it has cooked, directly from the casserole.

Agnello al fornello

Spit-roasted Lamb

A speciality of Moro in Matera.
The flavour of this dish depends on it being cooked in a special oven with an open fire. In olden days it was prepared by butchers and on the feast day of the Madonna of La Bruna, people travelled for many kilometres to eat it.
At Moro, host Don Peppino Giasi serves it as part of an arrosto misto (mixed roast) which also includes local sausage and involtini di agnello (lamb intestines wrapped around small pieces of liver). It is simple peasant cooking at its best.

1 whole lamb
salt

Clean the inside of the lamb and thread it on a spit. Cook it, turning constantly, until well browned. Salt the lamb three-quarters of the way through cooking and consume immediately upon removing from the spit. If necessary add more salt.

Capretto e carciofi
Kid with Artichokes

(If kid is not available, spring lamb may be used instead)

Serves 6

1.75 kg (3½ lb) leg of kid, boned
1 cup (8 fl oz) olive oil
60 g (2 oz) prosciutto, chopped
1 onion, finely chopped
4 tablespoons flour
1½ cups (12 fl oz) dry white wine
salt

freshly ground black pepper
6 fresh artichokes (if not in season
  canned artichokes may be used)
4 egg yolks
juice of 3 lemons
2 sprigs oregano, finely chopped
fresh parsley, finely chopped

1. Cut the meat into large dice.
2. In a heavy-bottomed casserole heat the oil, add the meat, prosciutto and onion. Sauté until the meat browns.
3. Sprinkle with flour and cook for a further 5 minutes.
4. Add the wine, salt and pepper, cover the casserole and cook for 45 minutes.
5. If fresh artichokes are used, cut them into four, remove the choke and add it to the casserole. Cook them for 15 minutes.
6. If canned artichokes are used they should be added to the meat just before serving as they do not require any cooking.
7. The total cooking time should be 1 to 1¼ hours or until the meat is tender.
8. Lightly beat the egg yolks and add pepper, salt and lemon juice.
9. Reduce the heat to very low and while stirring, pour the egg yolks into the sauce. Make sure that it does not boil otherwise the eggs will curdle.
10. Add the oregano and serve directly from the casserole sprinkled with chopped parsley.

Ciamotta
Deep Fried Vegetables

Serves 4-6

250 g (8 oz) eggplant (aubergine)
250 g (8 oz) potatoes
200 g (6½ oz) ripe tomatoes
3 large capsicums (peppers)

1 clove garlic
salt
freshly ground black pepper
olive oil for deep frying

1. Wash and slice the eggplant. Place the slices on a plate and sprinkle them with salt. Incline the plate and let it stand for one hour, so that the water from the eggplant runs off.
2. Wash the slices and dry them on a teatowel.
3. Peel the potatoes and cut them into cubes.
4. Immerse the tomatoes into boiling water, peel them and cut them into large cubes.
5. Cut the capsicums into halves, remove the seeds and cut them into strips.
6. In a saucepan heat the oil and lightly fry the eggplant slices and place them in a separate saucepan.
7. Partly fry the potatoes and the capsicum and add them to the eggplant.
8. Add the tomatoes, garlic, oil, salt and pepper. Mix everything well together and slowly cook for 1 hour.

Abruzzi e Molise

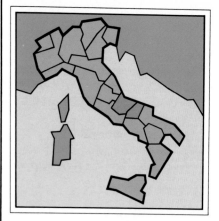

These two regions are mountainous and there is very little land available for agriculture. Most of the inhabitants are poor, many of them existing chiefly on vegetables and pasta.

The area boasts excellent pasta; the most famous is maccheroni alla chitarra (guitar macaroni), so called because it is cut into strips on a wooden frame with steel strings stretched across it, like a guitar. It is usually served with a meat sauce and grated pecorino cheese.

Polenta, usually connected with the cuisine of the north of Italy, is popular here too. The coastal cooking is naturally mostly dependent on fish.

Pickled fish is popular all over the area and on the coast a favourite way of cooking fish is to stuff it with breadcrumbs and herbs and bake it.

In the interior, the pig provides most of the specialities. In addition to fresh pork – especially porchetta (roast suckling pig) – Abruzzi makes many sausages. Two famous sausages from the capital city of L'Aquila are made from pig's liver. One is called sweet livers (fegati dolci) in which the liver is combined with honey. The other is crazy liver (fegati pazzi) where liver and hot pimentoes are combined.

The interior also provides freshwater fish, mostly trout, which are cooked in a very southern way with garlic, capers, parsley, olive oil and breadcrumbs.

Scamorza is a local cheese. It is similar to mozzarella in texture but formed into an egg shape. It is quite often threaded onto skewers and roasted over a fire. The outside takes on a dark yellow colour and the inside becomes soft and creamy.

Pescara, the only coastal city, is also the only place in the region where good food can be found. It even boasts a Guida Michelin one-star restaurant.

Church of Sacred Heart in Pescara, the capital of the Abruzzi.

Mozzarella in carrozza
Toasted Mozzarella Sandwich

Serves 4

8 slices white bread, crusts trimmed
4 slices mozzarella cheese
1-1½ cups (8-12 fl oz) milk
flour

2 eggs
salt
2 tablespoons butter
½ cup (4 fl oz) olive oil

1. Dip the slices of bread in the milk, but do not get them too wet.
2. Place one slice of cheese between two slices of bread.
3. Cut each sandwich diagonally in half, flour them lightly and dip them in the beaten eggs.
4. Fry the sandwiches in the butter-oil mixture until brown on both sides. Drain on kitchen paper.
5. Serve on a heated platter.

Maccheroni alla chitarra
Abruzzi Egg Noodles

Serves 4

500 g (1 lb) chitarra-type noodles
salt
water

SAUCE:
1 tablespoon butter
¼ cup (2 fl oz) olive oil

500 g (1 lb) lamb, minced
2 green peppers (capsicums), chopped
salt
¼ cup (2 fl oz) dry white wine
2 ripe tomatoes, peeled and chopped

1. Boil the noodles in salted water for 8 to 10 minutes and serve with the following sauce.
2. Heat the butter and the oil and fry the meat, stirring until brown. Add the peppers and the salt.
3. Add the wine and simmer until it has almost evaporated.
4. Add the tomatoes and simmer for ½ hour or until they have reduced to a thick sauce.
5. To serve, mix the sauce into the noodles.

Scrippelle 'mbusse
Abruzzi Stuffed Pancakes

Serves 4

½ cup (2 oz) flour
1 teaspoon salt
2 eggs
1 cup (8 fl oz) water
¼ cup (2 fl oz) olive oil
1 cup (4 oz) grated Parmesan or
  pecorino cheese

½ cup (2½ oz) chopped prosciutto
  ham
½-1 cup (4-8 fl oz) chicken stock
salt
freshly ground black pepper

1. Combine the flour, salt, eggs and water to form a smooth creamy batter.
2. Put a few drops of oil in a pancake pan and heat.
3. Pour sufficient of the batter into the pan to make a thin pancake. Fry on both sides until golden-brown. Continue in this way until you have used all the batter.
4. Preheat the oven to 120°C (250°F/Gas ½).
5. Mix the cheese with the prosciutto. Place equal amounts of it on each pancake, roll them and place the rolled pancakes beside each other in a buttered oven-proof dish.
6. Boil the chicken stock and pour over the pancakes to about ¾ of their depth.
7. Cover the dish and place it in the preheated oven for approximately 20 minutes.
8. Season and serve when the stock has been partially absorbed.

Cuscinetti di Teramo
Cushions of Teramo

Serves 4-6

2 cups (8 oz) flour
½ teaspoon salt
2 teaspoons sugar
3 tablespoons olive oil

½-¾ cup (4-6 fl oz) dry white wine
½-¾ cup (4-6 fl oz) thick jam or
  marmalade

1. Combine the flour, salt, sugar, oil and wine and make a firm but tender dough. Knead it and roll it out very thin.
2. Cut out circles 9 cm (3¼ in) in diameter and on each, place a teaspoon of the jam or marmalade. Fold the circles in half and press the edge firmly together.
3. Arrange the turnovers on a floured board and stand for 3 to 4 hours to dry the pasta.
4. Deep-fry them in hot oil 190°C (375°F) until they are golden in colour. Drain them on absorbent paper and serve them hot.

Apulia

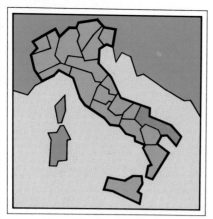

   While no part of the Apulia is far from the sea, there is a distinct inland cooking tradition which differs from that of the shores.

   The seafood of the region is excellent and appears in innumerable dishes. In fact the cuisine of the coastal towns consists almost exclusively of fish: red mullet, sardines, eel, mussels and anchovies.

   Taranto is famous for its oysters and there are countless recipes using them. But to me, Taranto oysters are best when eaten natural and ungarnished.

   A speciality of Brindisi is fresh anchovies, covered with chopped parsley and breadcrumbs and baked. Mussels and potatoes, a famous combination, could well have originated in Apulia where both are in abundance. Mussels feature in much of Apulia's cuisine: soups, fritters, salads, with rice and stuffed and baked.

   The seafood spaghetti of Taranto is renowned throughout Italy.

   Lamb and kid are favourite meats, and as the country is not very rich, every part of the animal finds its way into the pot. Offal appears in many regional dishes, one of the best known being the gniummerieddi of Martina Franca, where the intestines of the lamb or kid are wrapped around pieces of liver, heart or kidney, and then roasted over an open fire. Lamb roasted on a spit over an open fire is also a great delicacy. The only meat that can be called abundant in Apulia is game, and even then it is only eaten in certain areas, most notably Foggia.

   As everywhere else in the south, tubular pasta is very popular, especially the delicate handmade fusilli, where pieces of pasta are rolled around knitting needle-like rods.

Martina Franca at sunset.

Spaghetti Apulia Style

1 SPAGHETTI CON I BROCCOLI
Spaghetti with Broccoli

Serves 4

4 anchovy fillets
750 g (1½ lb) broccoli flowerets,
  trimmed
salt

375 g (12 oz) spaghetti
4 tablespoons olive oil
1 clove garlic, crushed

1. Chop the anchovies coarsely.
2. Steam or boil the broccoli in salted water but do not overcook it. (If boiling, keep the water for the spaghetti).
3. Cook the spaghetti 'al dente'.
4. While the spaghetti is cooking, heat the oil in a frying pan, and add the chopped anchovies and the garlic. With the back of a fork, mash the anchovies into a thick sauce.
5. Mix the broccoli with the anchovy sauce and pour it over the spaghetti. Serve immediately.

2 SPAGHETTI CON LE SEPPIE
Spaghetti with Squid or Cuttlefish

Serves 4

500 g (1 lb) squid or cuttlefish
1 onion, chopped
1 stalk celery, chopped
1 clove garlic, crushed
1 carrot, chopped
4 tablespoons olive oil

salt
freshly ground black pepper
¾ cup (6 fl oz) dry white wine
2 cups (16 fl oz) meat stock
3 tablespoons parsley, chopped

1. Clean the squid or the cuttlefish and slice it. Canned squid may be used.
2. Sauté the onion, celery, garlic and carrot in the oil, season, simmer for a few minutes and add the squid or cuttlefish.
3. Add the wine and cook until it has almost evaporated. Gradually add the stock and continue cooking for 1 hour.
4. Just before serving add the parsley. To serve, mix it with the previously cooked spaghetti.

3 SPAGHETTI ALLA SANGIOVANNIELLO
Spaghetti with Anchovies and Tomatoes

Serves 4

5-7 tinned peeled tomatoes
3 anchovy fillets, coarsely chopped
4 tablespoons olive oil
1 clove garlic, crushed
3 basil leaves, chopped
1 small piece hot chilli pepper,
  chopped

salt
3 tablespoons parsley, chopped
1 tablespoon capers, chopped
12 black olives, pitted

1. Purée the tomatoes.
2. With the back of a fork, mash the anchovies in the heated oil.
3. Add the garlic, basil and chilli and simmer until the sauce is thick but not dry. Remove the chilli when the sauce is hot enough for your taste. If the sauce is too thick, add a little of the spaghetti cooking water.
4. Just before serving, add the parsley, capers and olives. Mix the sauce into the previously-cooked spaghetti.

Fave in bianco
Purée of Fresh Broad Beans

From Ai Portici in Martina Franca.

Serves 4

500 g (1 lb) shelled white broad beans
salt
3-4 small potatoes, cut into large
  pieces
½ cup (4 fl oz) olive oil

1. Place the beans in a heavy cast-iron casserole. Add cold water and bring it slowly to the boil. Boil for approximately 5 minutes. Drain and rinse the beans.
2. Add the potatoes to the beans in the pan and cover with fresh water.
3. Simmer until the water has evaporated.
4. Pour the olive oil into the beans and potatoes and mash them like mashed potatoes.
5. The beans and potatoes may be served either hot or cold.

Melanzane al forno
Roasted Eggplant

From Ai Portici in Martina Franca.

Serves 4

4 medium-sized eggplants (aubergines)
½ cup (1 oz) fine soft breadcrumbs
½ cup (2 oz) grated pecorino cheese
4 tablespoons black olives, seeded and
  sliced
½ cup (4 fl oz) olive oil
2 tablespoons capers, washed
¼ cup chopped parsley

1. Preheat the oven to 200°C (400°F/Gas 6).
2. Cut each eggplant in half horizontally and remove the flesh with a spoon, making sure that the outside is not damaged.
3. With a knife, finely chop the eggplant flesh and place in a heavy cast-iron dish.
4. Add the breadcrumbs, half the cheese, and the olives. Mix well and fry in a little oil.
5. In a separate saucepan boil the empty eggplant shells in salted water for 10 minutes. Arrange them in a baking dish and moisten them with olive oil.
6. To the fried mixture add the capers, parsley and remaining oil. Mix the ingredients well together.
7. Fill the eggplant shells with this mixture and top it with some of the remaining grated cheese.
8. Place the dish in the preheated oven and bake for 20 to 30 minutes.
9. Stuffed eggplant may be served either hot or cold.

Zucchini in marinata
Marinated Zucchini

From Ai Portici in Martina Franca.

Serves 4

8 firm and large zucchinis (courgettes), sliced
1 cup (8 fl oz) olive oil

2-4 cups (16-32 fl oz) vinegar
salt
1 tablespoon finely chopped red chilli

1. Brown the zucchinis a few at a time in the oil.
2. Place the fried zucchinis in a dish (not aluminium).
3. Heat sufficient vinegar to cover the zucchinis, add salt and the chilli to taste.
4. When the vinegar boils, pour it over the zucchinis.
5. Allow to cool, place in a glass jar and preserve for serving.

Peperoni sott'aceto
Pickled Peppers

From Ai Portici in Martina Franca.

large firm peppers (capsicums)
white wine vinegar

1. Cut the peppers into quarters, wash them and remove their stems and seeds.
2. Dry and spread them out on a tray in the sun for a few hours.
3. Place them in a glass jar, cover with the vinegar and stand in a cool place for 2 to 3 days before using them.

Seppie ripiene
Stuffed Cuttlefish

From Al Gambero in Taranto, a stark, rather uninviting looking restaurant which serves excellent seafood. One could make a meal just by eating the antipasti: seafood salads of all kinds; stuffed, crumbed and fried mussels; calamari; prawns; lobster. Their pasta with various seafood sauces are also delicious.

Serves 4

750 g (1½ lb) small cuttlefish
345 g (11 oz) mussels
345 g (11 oz) small squid, cleaned and finely chopped
¾-1 cup (1½-2 oz) fine soft breadcrumbs

¼ cup (1 oz) grated pecorino cheese
1 tablespoon capers, finely chopped
2 eggs
2 tablespoons olive oil
salt
freshly ground pepper

1. Preheat the oven to 160°C (325°F/Gas 3).
2. Clean and empty the cuttlefish and wash them well.
3. With a sharp knife open the mussels and detach the mollusc. Chop them finely.
4. Place the mussels and squid in a bowl, add the breadcrumbs, pecorino, capers and eggs. Mix together well.
5. Fill the cuttlefish with this mixture. Be careful not to overfill or they will burst.
6. Place on a baking dish, sprinkle with oil and season with salt and pepper.
7. Place in the preheated oven and cook for ½ to ¾ hour. Serve hot.

Ai Portici, Martina Franca

Martina Franca is a fine jewel among the many beautiful towns of Italy. Splendidly preserved and immaculately maintained, it is one of the prettiest towns I have ever visited. Ai Portici has a modest entrance off one of the elegant baroque squares. Its basement location gives it a cosy atmosphere. Here, in contrast to the towns located along the shores, where the seafood is at its best, meat and especially lamb can be tried. The owner-chef cooks his lamb on a spit (right) in an oven fired with charcoal. The results are delicious. Spicy local sausages get the same treatment. Ai Portici serves a wide range of local cheeses, one of the most interesting is scamorza, similar to mozzarella, which is roasted on skewers with pieces of smoked bacon.

Above: *clockwise from bottom left: marinated zucchini (see p.62); pickled octopus (see p.64); fried peppers.*

Cozze ripiene al sugo

Stuffed Mussels in Tomato Sauce

From Al Gambero in Taranto.

Serves 4

1 kg (2 lb) mussels
3 tablespoons olive oil
2 cloves garlic
4 fresh tomatoes, peeled and puréed
¼ cup finely chopped basil

2 eggs, lightly beaten
2 tablespoons finely chopped parsley
sufficient soft breadcrumbs to make a
 firm but moist stuffing
salt
freshly ground black pepper

1. Scrub the mussels.
2. With the sharp edge of a knife, open the raw mussels without damaging the shells.
3. In the oil, fry one clove of garlic and when brown remove it. Add the tomato purée and sufficient water to cover the mussels.
4. Add the basil and cook the mixture for a few minutes.
5. Prepare the filling by mixing together the beaten eggs, parsley, the remaining garlic clove, finely chopped, and the breadcrumbs.
6. Place a little of the mixture on each mussel in its shell. Press the shells together to close and tie white thread around them to keep the two shells together.
7. Place the mussels in the sauce, which by now should be cooked.
8. Simmer the mussels for 15 to 20 minutes.
9. Remove the thread from the mussels and serve with boiled rice and the sauce.

Polpi sott'aceto

Pickled Octopus

From Ai Portici in Martina Franca.
Octopus prepared in this way can be served as an hors-d'oeuvre or as part of a fish salad.

1 kg (2 lb) fresh octopus, cleaned and
 tenderised
12 fresh mint leaves

3 cloves garlic, sliced into thin slivers
2 cups (16 fl oz) white wine vinegar

1. Place the octopus in boiling unsalted water and cook for approximately 1 hour, or until it feels tender when pierced with a fork.
2. Drain and slice it into 5 to 10 cm (2 to 4 in) pieces.
3. Dry the octopus and place in a glass jar, interleaving it with mint leaves and thin slivers of garlic. Cover with vinegar, seal the jar and preserve until ready to use.

Sogliole al piatto
Steamed Sole

Serves 4-6

1 kg (2 lb) fillets of sole
2 tablespoons parsley, chopped
2 cloves garlic, crushed
salt

freshly ground black pepper
4-5 tablespoons olive oil
4-6 segments of lemon

1. If a vegetable or asparagus steamer is not available, place the fillets of sole on a heatproof plate, sprinkle them with the parsley, garlic, salt, pepper and olive oil.
2. Place the plate on a rack in a casserole in some boiling water. Cover it and continue boiling the water for 3 to 5 minutes until the fish is steamed.
3. Serve with the lemon segments.

Agnello alla cacciatora
Lamb stew with Tomatoes and Potatoes

Serves 4

4 tablespoons olive oil
1 onion, chopped
800 g (1 lb 10 oz) lamb meat from the leg, cut into large cubes
500 g (1 lb) ripe tomatoes, peeled and chopped

400 g (13 oz) potatoes, peeled and cut into chunks
1 tablespoon dried oregano
salt
freshly ground black pepper

1. Preheat oven to 160°C (325°F/Gas 3).
2. Heat the oil in a heavy casserole and lightly sauté the onion.
3. Add the lamb, tomatoes, potatoes, oregano, salt and pepper.
4. Cover and cook in the preheated oven for 1½ hours, mixing the ingredients from time to time.

Ricotta fritta
Fried Ricotta

Serves 4

2 eggs
500 g (1 lb) ricotta, in one piece
2 tablespoons flour

oil for frying
100 g (3½ oz) sugar

1. Whip the eggs in a bowl.
2. Carefully, so as not to break it up, cut the ricotta into slices 1 cm (½ in) thick.
3. Dust the pieces with flour, dip them in the eggs and fry in the oil until golden brown.
4. Serve hot sprinkled with sugar.

Umbria

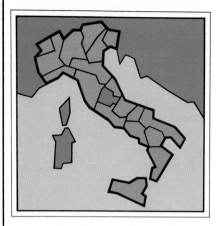

Whenever I think of Umbria, I have in mind pleasant things, mostly edible. The delicious chocolates from Perugia, said to be the best in Italy; black truffles from Norcia (especially good in spaghetti alla norcina) and porchetta (suckling pig), heavily peppered and roasted with fennel.

The olive oil is of excellent quality, mushrooms grow in profusion and lamb is delicious. Chianina beef cattle, famous in Tuscany, are also raised here, especially in the area around Perugia.

There are many freshwater rivers and lakes in the region, which abound with trout, perch, pike and eel.

Wheat is grown in the fertile valleys and the area produces much pasta. One of the specialities of Umbria is paglia e fieno (straw and grass), a mixture of green and yellow noodles served with prosciutto and cream.

A rather strange Perugian speciality is bruschetta (garlic toast). It is made by spreading crushed garlic and olive oil on hot toast and sprinkling with pepper and salt. It is traditionally eaten during the olive picking and in Perugia there is a garlic toast festival (sagra della bruschetta) on the last Sunday in March every year.

Cakes and biscuits (cookies) are numerous, especially in and around Perugia.

Umbria is rugged country with most of its towns situated picturesquely around the tops of hills and mountains. The cities are ancient and Perugia in particular is a living museum of architectural styles: Etruscan, Gothic and Renaissance.

The wine most often associated with Umbria is Orvieto. It is a light and dry white wine, the only one the region produces that is well-known in other countries.

Piazza Matteotti in Perugia.

Minestra di passatelli dell'Umbrio
Consommé with Dumplings

You need a food processor to make this dish successfully.

Serves 8

500 g (1 lb) veal, finely minced	45 g (1½ oz) softened butter
375 g (12 oz) spinach, cooked and puréed	5 eggs
	pinch of nutmeg
60 g (2 oz) beef marrow, mashed	salt
1 cup (4 oz) grated Parmesan cheese	freshly ground black pepper
1 cup (4 oz) fine dry breadcrumbs	6 cups (1.5 litres) beef consommé

1. Put all the ingredients except the consommé into a food processor and purée to a very fine paste.
2. Place the mixture in a colander and press it through holes into the simmering consommé. Lightly boil for 5 minutes and serve with extra grated Parmesan cheese.

Soffrito
Also known as buttato, this is a type of mirepoix which is used in the preparation of stews, broths and vegetable soups.

1 onion	2 sprigs parsley
1 carrot	1 sprig fresh herbs
1 stalk celery or some celery leaves	60 g (2 oz) ham, diced
½-1 clove garlic	oil, butter or dripping

Finely chop all the vegetables and herbs and add the ham. Fry the mixture in the oil until brown.

Spaghetti con punte d'asparagi
Spaghetti with Asparagus Tips

Serves 4

1 kg (2 lb) fresh asparagus or 300 g (10 oz) canned asparagus tips	salt
	freshly ground black pepper
2½ tablespoons olive oil	350 g (11 oz) spaghetti
400 g (13 oz) fresh tomatoes, peeled and chopped	4 tablespoons grated Parmesan cheese

1. If using fresh asparagus, boil it in plenty of salted water or steam it for 10 minutes.
2. Cut off the tips about 4 cm (1½ in) long. Use the rest of the asparagus to make a cream of asparagus soup.
3. In a heavy casserole heat the oil, add the asparagus tips, tomatoes, pepper and salt.
4. Cook over low heat for 5 minutes.
5. Cook the spaghetti to taste in boiling salted water and serve with the sauce poured over it. Sprinkle with the grated cheese.

Pomodori ripieni

Stuffed Tomatoes

From La Rosetta in Perugia.

Serves 4

4 large tomatoes	salt
3 tablespoons olive oil	freshly ground black pepper
1 onion, chopped	¼ teaspoon nutmeg
1 tablespoon parsley, chopped	2 tablespoons fine dry breadcrumbs
3 tablespoons fresh breadcrumbs	for topping
2 teaspoons capers	2 tablespoons olive oil

1. Preheat the oven to 190°C (375°F/Gas 5).
2. Cut a slice from the base, not the stem end of the tomatoes and reserve. Hollow out the centres. Reserve the flesh, discarding the juice and seeds.
3. Heat the oil in a frying pan and sauté the onion.
4. Remove the pan from the heat and add the parsley, fresh breadcrumbs, capers, salt, pepper, nutmeg and two tablespoons of the reserved tomato flesh.
5. Mix all the ingredients thoroughly and fill the tomatoes with the stuffing.
6. Replace the reserved tomato tops, coat the tomatoes with dry breadcrumbs and sprinkle them with oil.
7. Arrange them on an oiled shallow baking tray and bake them in the preheated oven for 30 minutes.

Spezzato di tacchino

Umbrian Casserole of Turkey with Olives

Serves 6

2 cloves garlic	1 small piece hot chilli, finely chopped
½ cup (4 fl oz) olive oil	(or a pinch of cayenne pepper)
1.5 kg (3 lb) turkey pieces	½ cup (4 fl oz) dry white wine
flour	24 black olives, pitted
salt	¾ cup (6 fl oz) beef stock

1. In a large heavy-bottomed frying pan, fry the garlic in olive oil until it is brown. Discard the garlic.
2. Sprinkle the turkey pieces with flour and brown them in the garlic-flavoured oil.
3. Add salt and the chilli, being careful not to use too much otherwise the dish will be too hot.
4. Transfer everything to a large casserole with a lid.
5. Add the wine, olives and the stock.
6. Cover and simmer on a low heat for 2 hours.
7. Serve the turkey pieces directly out of the casserole and mask them with the cooking juices.

Stufatino umbrese

Umbrian Beef Stew

Serves 6

2.25 kg (4½ lb) shin beef
2 tablespoons butter
2 onions, sliced
2 cloves garlic, crushed
90 g (3 oz) bacon, cut into strips
2 tablespoons chopped fresh marjoram
salt

freshly ground black pepper
1 cup (8 fl oz) red wine
4 tablespoons concentrated tomato
  purée
water
1 bunch celery
60 g (2 oz) butter

1. Cut the meat into thin slices.
2. In the butter, sauté the onions and garlic. When they are browned, add the bacon, marjoram, salt and pepper.
3. Add the pieces of meat and brown them slightly.
4. Pour in the wine and cook for a few minutes, then add the tomato purée and cook for another 3 to 4 minutes.
5. Add enough water to cover the meat.
6. Cover the pan and gently simmer the stew for 2 to 3 hours.
7. Shortly before serving, cut the celery into 2 cm (¾ in) pieces and gently braise it in the butter. Season it and serve the celery with the stew.

Scaloppine alla perugina

Veal Escalopes with Chicken Liver Croûtons, Perugina Style

Serves 4

500 g (1 lb) thin slices of veal, cut
  either from the fillet or the inside of
  the leg
½ cup (2 oz) flour
salt
freshly ground black pepper
juice 1 lemon

4 tablespoons butter
8 slices fresh French bread
½ cup (4 oz) clarified butter
2 slices ham, finely chopped
125 g (4 oz) chicken livers, finely
  chopped

1. Cut the veal into 5 cm (2 in) square slices, each weighing approximately 30 g (1 oz). Allow 3 to 4 slices per person.
2. Beat them flat, dust them with flour, season and sprinkle with half the lemon juice.
3. Fry them in half the butter, set them aside and keep them hot while preparing the chicken liver croûtons (crostini di fegato).
4. To prepare the chicken liver croûtons, fry the slices of bread in the clarified butter. Remove and drain.
5. Brown the ham lightly in the remaining butter, then add the livers and the rest of the lemon juice. Season, cover the pan and cook gently for 8 to 10 minutes.
6. Spread the liver on the fried bread. Arrange the croûtons around the sides of a preheated serving dish and place the escalopes in the centre.

La Rosetta, Perugia

Perugia is among my favourite towns in Italy and I very much like Umbrian cooking, especially anything labelled 'alla norcina', as this implies the use of the local black truffle.

My visit to La Rosetta was very rewarding. To start, there was the dry prosciutto di Perugia and then salame perugino, followed by spaghetti alla norcina. Umbrian lamb is particularly good when simply spit-roasted, and the porchetta perugiana was served cooked with fennel, coriander, garlic and freshly ground pepper. The meal was complemented by the dry white orvietto of the region.

Above: clockwise from bottom left: sweet bun of Saint Costanzo, Easter cheese bread, meringue cake.
Right: some of the many ingredients that go into Umbrian cooking, including a tin of the famous black truffles of Norcia.

Spiedini misti spoletani

Mixed Meat Kebabs

Serves 4

4 medallions of lamb
4 medallions of pork
4 pieces chicken breast, about 2.5 cm
  (1 in) square
4 pieces pork liver, about 2.5 cm (1 in)
  square
16 pieces bacon or speck, about
  2.5 cm (1 in) square

16 sage leaves
2 sprigs rosemary, chopped
½ cup (4 fl oz) olive oil
4 juniper berries, crushed
salt
freshly ground black pepper

1. Skewer the meat, alternating each slice with a piece of bacon or speck and sage leaves.
2. Arrange the skewers in a shallow porcelain or glass dish, sprinkle them with the rosemary. Pour over the oil and sprinkle them with juniper berries.
3. Let the skewers stand overnight to marinate.
4. Place the skewers under a hot grill and cook for 10 to 15 minutes, turning often, until the meat is cooked.
5. Serve them sprinkled with salt and pepper.

Abbacchio alla cacciatora

Lamb, Hunter's Style

Serves 6

1 kg (2 lb) stewing lamb, diced
2 tablespoons olive oil
salt
freshly ground black pepper
1 clove garlic, crushed
1 sprig fresh rosemary, chopped

2 fresh sage leaves
¼ cup (1 oz) flour
½ cup (4 fl oz) white wine vinegar
½-1 cup (4-8 fl oz) water
3 anchovy fillets, finely chopped

1. In a saucepan or cast iron casserole, brown the meat in the oil.
2. Season, add the garlic, rosemary and chopped sage leaves. Sprinkle with the flour and continue cooking for a few minutes.
3. Add the vinegar, water and anchovies.
4. Cook on a low heat until the meat is tender, approximately 45 minutes. Make sure the stew is quite moist, and if necessary add more water.
5. Serve with triangles of fried bread.

Granita di limone

Lemon granita

Serves 6

½ cup (4 oz) sugar
2 cups (16 fl oz) water
6-8 lemons to produce 1¼ cups

(10 fl oz) lemon juice
½ teaspoon grated lemon peel
6 half-slices lemon

1. Make a syrup from the sugar and the water and boil it for 5 minutes. Cool.
2. Mix in the lemon juice and lemon peel.
3. Pour the mixture into an ice-cube tray, place in the freezer and freeze until quite hard.
4. Remove from the tray and crush it with the handle of a knife.
5. Serve in individual glass dishes garnished with lemon slices.

Pinoccate di Perugia

Pine Nut Fondant

250 g (8 oz) pine nuts
1½ cups (11 oz) sugar
1 cup (8 fl oz) water

¾ cup (4 oz) candied orange peel, cut
  into small pieces
rice paper, cut into small squares

1. Place the pine nuts on a baking dish and put it into a low oven to crisp them without browning them.
2. In a saucepan, combine the sugar and the water. Bring it to the boil and without stirring, boil it to 160°C (325°F) on a sugar thermometer.
3. Pour the syrup into an enamel or stainless steel bowl and with a wooden spoon or palette knife, knead the mixture until it is opaque.
4. Add the nuts and orange peel.
5. With a wet teaspoon place small balls of the mixture on the rice paper and leave to cool.
6. Trim the rice paper to the shape of the mixture on top.
7. Serve sprinkled with icing (confectioners') sugar.

Tuscany

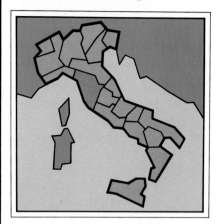

My first meal in Florence was at Buca Lapi, a restaurant in the cellars of the 15th Century Palazzo Antinori. It seemed a fitting place to start my tour because, since the late 14th Century, the name of the Antinori family has been associated with Chianti wine. It was from this very cellar that they first sold their wines to the public. Later, the Lapi family opened a restaurant in the cellar; descendants of the Lapi family still run the restaurant and descendants of the Antinori family still live in the upper floor of the palazzo. Appropriately my meal consisted of bistecca alla fiorentina, fagioli al olio and chianti classico Antinori. The steak came from the famous Chianina cattle and was a giant T-bone, grilled to underdone perfection. It is such simplicity and striving for classical perfection which characterises most of Tuscan cooking. They use the finest and freshest ingredients and cook them in the simplest possible ways, avoiding rich sauces and heavy seasoning. Tuscan vegetables are prepared with the same restraint. Asparagus, artichokes, spinach and large mushrooms appear regularly on Tuscan menus, often cooked in the superb olive oil of Lucca.

Siena is the home of panforte, that spiced sweet Christmas cake that is now known all over the world.

On the coast, clams, mussels, octopus, and red mullet are plentiful and find their way into many regional dishes. One of the most famous is cacciucco alla livornese, from the province of Leghorn. It is a fish soup, similar to the French bouillabaisse, which contains many types of fish as well as onions, garlic, parsley and tomatoes.

Inland, especially in the Maremma region, game abounds. Birds, rabbits, deer and wild boar are all used extensively in the cuisine of that region.

Palazzo Vecchio in Florence.

Zuppa di fagioli alla toscana

Tuscan Bean Soup

Serves 4

500 g (1 lb) white dried beans
6 cups (1.5 litres) water or beef stock
salt
freshly ground black pepper

2 tablespoons olive oil
1-2 cloves garlic, crushed
¼ cup chopped parsley

1. Wash the dried beans and soak them in the water or stock overnight.
2. Gently simmer the beans in the same water or stock for approximately 3 hours, or until they are soft.
3. When cooked, put half the beans in a food processor and purée them until they are fine in texture. If a processor is not available rub them through a sieve. Return the puréed beans to the saucepan and season.
4. In the olive oil lightly fry the garlic and the parsley.
5. Stir this mixture into the soup and serve hot with crusty bread.

Note: The traditional recipe calls for fresh oil to be poured into the soup before serving.

Triglie alla livornese

Red Mullet Leghorn Style

If red mullet is not available bream can also be prepared in this manner.

Serves 4

2 cloves garlic, crushed
1 onion, chopped
½ cup (4 fl oz) olive oil
500 g (1 lb) tomatoes, peeled and
    chopped

salt
freshly ground black pepper
4 small fish
½ cup (2 oz) flour
½ cup chopped parsley

1. Sauté the garlic and the onion in half the oil until golden-brown.
2. Add the tomatoes and cook gently for 15 minutes. Season.
3. Dust the fish with flour and separately fry them in the remaining oil. Pour off the excess fat and pour the sauce over the fish. Cook the fish in the sauce for a further 5 minutes. Serve sprinkled with parsley.

Torta di carciofi alla toscana

Artichoke Omelette, Tuscan Style

Serves 6

6 artichokes (use tinned artichokes if
    fresh ones not available)
2 tablespoons flour
30 g (1 oz) butter

6 eggs
salt
freshly ground black pepper
4 tablespoons milk

1. Preheat the oven to 190°C (375°F/Gas 5).
2. If using tinned artichokes, cut them in half and roll them in flour. If fresh, trim the leaves and boil them for 20 minutes in water with a little lemon juice. Remove the large outside leaves and scrape out the choke. You are left with a cone of light green leaves. Prepare them as above.
3. Butter a shallow oven-proof dish and place the artichokes in it.
4. Mix the eggs with the salt, pepper and milk and beat lightly.
5. Pour the mixture over the artichokes and bake in the pre-heated oven for approximately 10 minutes.

Uova alla fiorentina

Florentine Eggs

Serves 6

4 cups cooked chopped spinach (buy
  two bunches)
¼ cup (2 fl oz) melted butter
3 tablespoons flour
2 cups (16 fl oz) hot milk
salt

freshly ground black pepper
4 cups (1 litre) water
2 tablespoons vinegar
6 eggs
4 tablespoons grated Parmesan cheese

1. Preheat the oven to 200°C (400°F/Gas 6).
2. In an ovenproof dish, spread out the spinach which has been previously cooked and seasoned.
3. To prepare a Béchamel sauce, melt the butter in a saucepan, add the flour and cook for 2 to 3 minutes, stirring constantly. Add the hot milk, continue to stir for another 3 to 4 minutes and season the sauce.
4. Boil the water, add the vinegar and while simmering gently, carefully break the eggs into the water. Poach for 3 to 4 minutes.
5. With a perforated spoon, take the eggs out of the water and place them on top of the bed of spinach. Cover them with the Béchamel sauce and sprinkle with the Parmesan cheese.
6. Place the dish in the preheated oven and bake for 20 minutes.
  The dish can be placed under the grill until the surface is golden brown if desired.

Arselle alla maremmana

Pippies (Clams) Maremma Style

Pippies (clams) tend to be sandy and it is necessary to clean them. Place them in a large bowl filled with salted water and leave them to stand overnight. (1 tablespoon of salt per 4 cups (1 litre) of water).

Serves 4

6 tablespoons olive oil
2 cloves garlic, crushed
3 sprigs fresh sage, chopped
2 kg (4 lb) pippies (clams)
1 cup (8 fl oz) dry white wine
salt

freshly ground black pepper
2 eggs
juice 1 lemon
½ cup chopped parsley
12-16 1.5 cm (½ in) slices of fresh
  French bread

1. Put the olive oil, one of the garlic cloves and the sage in a large saucepan. Sauté for 3 to 4 minutes, then remove the garlic and sage.
2. Put the pippies in the saucepan, add the wine and season with salt and pepper. Cook over high heat for 5 minutes or until all the pippies are open.
3. Drain the pippies and remove them from their shells.
4. Return the pippies to the pan.
5. In a bowl, beat the eggs with the lemon juice and season.
6. Pour the mixture over the pippies, stir and remove from the heat.
7. Add the parsley and the remaining garlic.
8. Arrange the bread on heated plates and pour the pippi and egg mixture over them. (The bread may also be toasted.)

Pollo alla diavola

Chicken with Meat Sauce

This is the best known of Tuscan chicken dishes. It may appear a little complex but if you follow the three steps given here, you'll find it easy, and the effort is definitely worthwhile. The sauce is prepared in two stages: first a basic meat sauce which, although it is easy to prepare, will take 3 to 4 hours to cook. Then it is combined with the second stage of the sauce. The chicken is grilled and the sauce is spooned over it.

Serves 6

SALSA ALLA DIAVOLA
Sauce Diablo

STAGE 1:
2 stalks celery, chopped
2 onions, chopped
½ cup chopped parsley
3 tablespoons olive oil
1 clove garlic, crushed
2 sprigs fresh thyme, chopped
4 bay leaves
250 g (8 oz) beef, minced
250 g (8 oz) veal, minced
salt
freshly ground black pepper
1 cup (8 fl oz) water

STAGE 2:
1½ cups (12 fl oz) dry white wine
2 tablespoons vinegar
2 tablespoons chopped spring onions
  (scallions)
2 sprigs fresh thyme
1 bay leaf
12 black peppercorns, crushed
salt
3 cups (24 fl oz) sauce from Stage 1
2 tablespoons chopped parsley
3 tablespoons chopped fresh ginger
4 tablespoons butter

CHICKEN:
3 chickens, about 600 g (1 lb 3 oz)
  each
½ cup (4 fl oz) olive oil

salt
freshly ground black pepper

Sauce, Stage 1
1. In a saucepan fry the celery, onions and parsley in the oil until lightly browned.
2. Add the garlic, thyme and bay leaves. Cook for 3 minutes.
3. Add the beef and the veal. Cook gently, stirring constantly until the meat is well browned.
4. Add the water and season.
5. Gently simmer for 3½ hours, occasionally adding more water to make sure that it does not dry out.
6. When the sauce is cooked, put it in a blender or food processor and process until it is fine in texture.

Sauce, Stage 2
1. In a saucepan combine the wine, vinegar, spring onions, thyme, bay leaf, peppercorns and salt.
2. Boil until it has reduced to one-third of its original volume.
3. Add the meat sauce from Stage 1 and continue cooking for 2 to 3 minutes.
4. Put the sauce in a blender or food processor and process until it is fine in texture.
5. Return to the saucepan and while gently simmering, add the parsley, ginger and butter. Taste, and if necessary adjust the seasoning.

The Chicken
1. Cut the chickens along the breastbone and flatten them with a cleaver.
2. Brush the chickens with the olive oil and place them under a preheated grill. (Make sure they are not too near the heat otherwise they may burn before they are cooked.) They will take 10 to 15 minutes each side. During the grilling, brush the chickens with the oil.
3. When the chickens are cooked, sprinkle with pepper and salt and serve half a chicken per person, masked with the diablo sauce.

Buca Lapi, Florence

Buca Lapi is situated in the basement of the Antinori Palace where the Antinori family (of Chianti wine fame), after more than five centuries, still resides. It is a pity that the vaulted ceilings of the ancient cellars have been spoiled by tourist posters; nevertheless, the food is good and many of the dishes served there are traditionally Florentine. Probably the best example of Florentine food is bistecca alla fiorentina, chianina beef grilled over charcoal and served with a simple dish of fagioli al olio (Tuscan white beans in oil). Naturally this is accompanied by Chianti classico Antinori from the landlord's cellar.

Above: *panforte (see p.81).*

Bistecca alla fiorentina
Steak Florentine Style

From Buca Lapi in Florence.
This dish is a very simple one and its main character depends on the use of the best quality beef and cooking it over charcoal.

Serves 4

1 large T-bone steak (approx. 1 kg
  (2 lb) in weight)

salt
pepper

1. If a charcoal fire is not available, grill the meat on both sides, turning it from time to time until it is well browned but rare inside.
2. Sprinkle with salt and pepper before serving.

Fritto misto alla fiorentina
Mixed Fry in the Florentine Manner

A tasty combination of vegetables, offal, meat and chicken, deep fried and served sprinkled with lemon juice. It is best served to a large number of people.

Serves 6-8

BATTER:
2½ cups (10 oz) flour
1 teaspoon finely chopped fresh
  rosemary
salt
pepper
4 eggs, separated
¼ teaspoon nutmeg
1-1½ cups (8-12 fl oz) dry white wine

6-8 small artichokes or artichoke
  hearts (tinned may be used)
2 lambs' brains

2 calves' sweetbreads
water
4 tablespoons vinegar
oil for deep frying
2 cups calves' liver, cut into large dice
6-8 lamb cutlets (without any fat)
3-4 chicken fillets, cut into large dice
3 zucchinis (courgettes) cut into thick
  slices
315 g (10 oz) cauliflower, separated
  into small flowerets
juice 2-3 lemons

1. To prepare the batter, in a mixing bowl, combine the flour, rosemary, salt and pepper. Add, while stirring constantly, the egg yolks, nutmeg and sufficient wine to make the batter the consistency of thick cream. Stir until smooth. Refrigerate for 1 hour.
2. Cut the artichokes in half.
3. Blanch the brains and the sweetbreads in the water and vinegar for 5 minutes, season. Drain them and cool under cold running water. Peel the membranes. Slice into 2 cm (¾ in) slices.
4. Just before frying, whip the egg whites until they are stiff and fold them into the batter.
5. Heat the oil to 190°C (375°F).
6. Dip the meats (and offals) into the batter and fry them first for 3 minutes, then dip the vegetables in the batter and add them to the deep-frier and continue to fry for a further 3 minutes.
7. When cooked, remove the pieces from the pan, drain and serve on individual plates sprinkled with lemon juice.

Note: If a deep frier is not available, the frying can be done in 2 frying pans, the meats in one for 5 to 6 minutes, the vegetables in the other for 2 to 3 minutes.

Zampa alla fiorentina

Calves' Shank Stew, Florentine Style

Serves 6

3 calves' shanks
3 bay leaves
12 peppercorns
1 carrot, chopped
1 stalk celery, chopped
1 onion, chopped

salt and pepper
water
2 cups (16 fl oz) meat sauce (see Stage 1, pollo alla diavola, page 78)
½ cup (2 oz) grated Parmesan cheese

1. In a large saucepan place the calves' shanks, bay leaves, carrot, celery, onion, salt and pepper. Cover with water.
2. Simmer for 2 hours until the meat is tender and comes easily off the bone. Remove the meat from the pan.
3. Chop the meat into small dice and put it into a shallow gratin dish. Add the meat sauce and half of the Parmesan cheese.
4. Sprinkle the rest of the cheese on top, place it under the grill until golden-brown. Serve in the gratin dish.

Note: The water in which the shanks have been cooked will have turned into a delicious stock which may be used for the preparation of a soup or sauce.

Panforte

Traditional Christmas Cake from Siena

Makes 1 cake approximately 45 x 38 cm (18 x 15 in)

200 g (6½ oz) blanched almonds
100 g (3½ oz) hazelnuts, roasted
100 g (3½ oz) glacé citron
100 g (3½ oz) glacé pumpkin
100 g (3½ oz) glacé melon rind
100 g (3½ oz) dried figs
155 g (5 oz) walnut kernels

30 g (1 oz) sweet cocoa (or drinking chocolate)
10 g (⅓ oz) powdered cinnamon
10 g (⅓ oz) mixed spices
⅓ cup (4 oz) honey
155 g (5 oz) caster (powdered) sugar
2 sheets rice paper

1. Preheat the oven to 180°C (350°F/Gas 4).
2. Finely chop all ingredients up to and including the walnut kernels.
3. Put them in a bowl, add the cocoa, half of the cinnamon and the mixed spices. Mix well together.
4. Put the honey and all but a tablespoon of the caster sugar in a saucepan. Heat and stir constantly until a drop of the mixture solidifies in contact with cold water.
5. Remove from the heat and add the nut-fruit mixture; mix well together.
6. Line the bottom of a shallow baking dish with one of the sheets of rice paper and pour the mixture on top of it. Cover with the other sheet.
7. Place in the preheated oven and bake for 30 minutes.
8. Remove from the oven, cool, unmould and sprinkle with the remaining caster sugar and cinnamon.
9. Do not serve until the next day. With a sharp knife cut it into bite-sized pieces.

Note: If glacé pumpkin and melon rind are not available, use other glacé fruits such as peaches or pineapple.

Emilia-Romagna

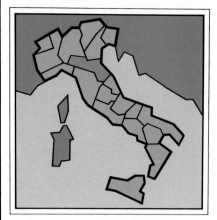

Emilia-Romagna is the home of some of Italy's most famous products: Parmesan cheese, Parma ham (prosciutto), mortadella sausage and tagliatelle. Tortellini and lasagna are also said to have been invented in Emilia-Romagna.

It is an area especially rich in raw materials. On the Adriatic coast, fish is plentiful and varied. Sturgeon, hake, mullet, mackerel, cuttlefish, squid, oysters, clams, scallops are all found here as are many others with local dialect names. Comacchio is famous for its eels and Ravenna for brodetto, a type of mixed fish stew.

Inland, fruit is plentiful and of excellent quality, especially apples and pears. Sugar beets, asparagus, zucchinis and potatoes all grow in abundance. The wheat which grows here is made into high quality pasta and cows which are fed on grass and clover produce thick creamy milk from which Parmesan cheese is made. The whey from the milk is fed to the pigs which in turn produce Parma ham and mortadella.

Bologna is the capital of the province and it is responsible for many of the region's most famous dishes: Bolognese sauce or ragu; costolette alla bolognese (thin slices of veal, crumbed and cooked with Parma ham and Parmesan cheese); filetti di tacchino alla bolognese (turkey breasts cooked in the same way); and involtini which are slices of veal wrapped around a meat stuffing and cooked in Bolognese sauce.

But many of the other cities in the region have their own specialities.

Modena produces zampone, a sausage made from stuffed pigs' feet, much appreciated all over Italy, cotechino, a cylindrical sausage and amaretti, those delicious little macaroons which are packed into beautiful tins and exported all over the world.

The Parma area produces Parmesan cheese, Parma ham, tomato paste and many pork sausages.

Emilia-Romagna is a region of rich and hearty food, almost as much loved in other parts of Italy, and indeed in the rest of the world, as it is in its home territory.

Statue of Emporer Augustus outside Sant Apolinare in Ravenna.

CESARE AUGUSTO
IMPERATORE

FONDATORE DEL PORTO
DI CLASSE

Minestra di passatelli

Chicken Consommé with Passatelli

Serves 4

4 eggs
1⅓ cups (5 oz) grated Parmesan
   cheese
4 tablespoons fine soft breadcrumbs
60 g (2 oz) butter, softened

salt
freshly ground black pepper
¼ teaspoon nutmeg
4 cups (1 litre) chicken consommé

1. Mix together in a bowl, the eggs, ¾ cup grated Parmesan, breadcrumbs, butter, salt, pepper and nutmeg.
2. Beat the mixture well until it forms a paste. Put the mixture into a saucepan and heat it over a low flame for 2 minutes.
3. Using a colander or perforated draining spoon, press the paste through it into the simmering consommé. Cook for only 1 or 2 minutes. The paste will form into short spaghetti-type pieces called passatelli.
4. Serve the soup sprinkled with the remaining Parmesan.

Lasagna all ferrarese

Lasagna Ferrara Style

Serves 4

1 onion, chopped
1 carrot, chopped
1 stick celery, chopped
3 tablespoons butter
1 cup (5 oz) prosciutto, chopped
250 g (8 oz) beef, minced
1 cup (8 fl oz) dry white wine
2½ cups (1¼ lb) tinned peeled
   tomatoes, chopped
salt

freshly ground black pepper
375 g (12 oz) lasagna noodles
1½ cups (6 oz) grated Parmesan
   cheese
BECHAMEL SAUCE:
2 tablespoons butter
2 tablespoons flour
1½-2 cups (12-16 fl oz) hot milk
¼ teaspoon nutmeg

1. Sauté the onion, carrot and celery in the butter, add the prosciutto and cook for 6 minutes.
2. Add the minced beef and brown, stirring constantly.
3. Add the wine and cook until it has almost completely evaporated.
4. Add the tomatoes, season, lower the heat and simmer for 1 hour. If too much of the liquid evaporates add some water.
5. Cook the lasagna in plenty of salted water; when still quite firm, remove it from the heat and rinse it in cold water.
6. Preheat the oven to 200°C (400°F/Gas 6).
7. Make the Béchamel: In a saucepan melt the butter, add the flour and, stirring constantly, cook for 5 minutes. Add the hot milk and cook for 10 to 15 minutes, stirring occasionally. Season and add the nutmeg.
8. Grease an ovenproof dish and arrange alternate layers of lasagna, meat sauce, and, Béchamel, sprinkled with some of the Parmesan. Finish off at the top with a layer of Béchamel sprinkled with the rest of the cheese.
9. Bake in the preheated oven for 30 to 45 minutes.

Tortellini alla bolognese

Tortellini Bolognese Style

Tortellini are amongst the most famous dishes of Bologna. They are little turban-like pasta coils filled with various types of stuffings served either dry, in broth or with sauces. This recipe is from Al Catunzein in Bologna.

Serves 4

PASTA:
500 g (1 lb) flour
3 eggs
salt
water

STUFFING:
30 g (1 oz) butter
90 g (3 oz) lean pork, finely chopped
60 g (2 oz) lean veal, finely chopped
60 g (2 oz) breast of chicken, finely chopped

60 g (2 oz) ham, finely chopped
60 g (2 oz) mortadella, finely chopped
60 g (2 oz) veal brains, blanched and finely chopped
salt
freshly ground black pepper
¾ cup (3 oz) grated Parmesan cheese
2 eggs
1 teaspoon nutmeg

Pasta

1. Place the flour in a mound on a floured board. Make a well in the centre and break the eggs into it. Add a teaspoon of salt and about 4 tablespoons of water. Fold the flour over the eggs and knead with your hands until the eggs, water and flour are properly mixed and can be formed into a ball. Continue to knead with the palm of your right hand while holding the dough with your left. Continue this for 10 minutes. From time to time flour your hand and the board.
2. Divide the dough in half. Roll out one half with a rolling pin, wrap it around the rolling pin and each time stretch it a little more. Sprinkle the dough with flour after each rolling. After 10 to 12 times the pasta should be so thin that it is almost transparent. Lay it out on a table or hang it over the back of a chair while you proceed with the second piece of dough in the same manner. Allow the dough to rest for 30 minutes.
3. Cut it into rounds of about 4 cm (1½ in) in diameter in readiness for the stuffing.

Stuffing

1. Melt the butter and sauté the pork, veal and chicken until light brown. Add the ham, mortadella and brains. Season, cover and simmer for 15 minutes. If the texture is not fine enough, put it through a food processor or meat mincer.
2. Add the cheese, eggs and nutmeg, and if necessary, adjust the seasoning.
3. Place ½ teaspoon of stuffing on the previously cut rounds of pasta. Fold each round with the top edge just short of the bottom. Bring the two points of the disc together, curling the tortellini around the finger to form a little ring.
4. Place the completed tortellini on a floured board, cover with a cloth and let them stand until the next day.
5. Poach them either in salted water or chicken or beef stock for 4 minutes.
6. Serve them with melted butter sprinkled with grated Parmesan cheese.

Costolette alla bolognese
Cutlets Bolognese Style

This recipe comes from the restaurant Nerina in Bologna. It is a large restaurant, situated in a cellar, right in the centre of Bologna. It specialises in regional cookery and is famous for its collection of Italian wines, especially those from Emilia-Romagna.

Serves 4

½ onion, sliced
4 tablespoons olive oil
250 g (8 oz) tomatoes, peeled and
  mashed
salt
freshly ground black pepper
4 slices veal, approximately 100 g
  (3½ oz) each

flour, enough to dust the meat
2 eggs beaten lightly
breadcrumbs, enough to coat the meat
70 g (2½ oz) butter
4 slices raw ham (prosciutto)
4 slices Parmesan cheese

1. Preheat the oven to 190°C (375°F/Gas 5).
2. Lightly sauté the onion in the oil for approximately 5 minutes.
3. Add the tomatoes, salt and pepper and cook for 30 minutes over a low heat.
4. Flatten out the meat until very thin, dust with flour and dip first in the beaten egg and then in the breadcrumbs.
5. In a frying pan, melt the butter and fry the meat until golden brown on both sides.
6. Grease a baking dish and arrange the meat on it.
7. Top each slice of meat with a slice of prosciutto and a slice of Parmesan. Sprinkle lightly with pepper, pour over the tomato sauce and place the dish in the oven for 5 to 7 minutes. Serve hot.

Ragù alla bolognese
Bolognese Meat Sauce

This famous sauce may be used with any type of pasta.

Serves 6

90 g (3 oz) bacon, chopped
1 tablespoon butter
1 onion, chopped
1 carrot, chopped
1 stalk celery, chopped
250 g (8 oz) beef, minced
125 g (4 oz) chicken livers, chopped
2 tablespoons concentrated tomato
  purée

1 cup (8 fl oz) dry white wine
salt
freshly ground black pepper
¼ teaspoon nutmeg
1 cup (8 fl oz) beef stock
½-1 cup (4-8 fl oz) cream (optional)

1. Brown the bacon in the butter, add the onion, carrot, and celery and sauté until brown.
2. Add the meat and stir well to make sure that it is evenly browned.
3. Add the chicken livers, cook for 3 to 4 minutes, then add the tomato purée and the wine. Season and add the nutmeg and stock.
4. Cover and simmer for 30 to 40 minutes.
5. Just before serving, add the cream, if used.
6. To serve, pour the sauce over previously cooked pasta.

Al Catunzein, Bologna

I had a wonderful meal at Al Catunzein, starting with an antipasto of Bologna's most famous product: the mortadella. Then came tiny servings of different types of home-made pasta: green stricchetti with prosciutto, butter and Parmesan; tortelloni stuffed with ricotta and parsley and served in a cream and prosciutto sauce; garganelli with mushrooms; lasagna made with minced beef and prosciutto (above), and best of all, tortellini stuffed with Parmesan, turkey meat, veal, mortadella and nutmeg. And this was only the first course.

Right: *mortadella, surrounded by other typical local sausages.*

Bomba di riso
Pigeon and Rice

A classic dish of Piancenza, in which the pigeon is served in a mound of rice with a mushroom sauce and it is finished in the oven. A young spatchcock may be used instead.

Serves 4

2 onions, sliced
4 tablespoons butter
2 pigeons or spatchcocks
2 chicken livers, chopped
125 g (4 oz) chicken giblets, chopped
125 g (4 oz) chopped mushrooms
2 tablespoons concentrated tomato
 purée

1 cup (8 fl oz) dry white wine
salt
freshly ground black pepper
4 cups (1 litre) beef or chicken stock
1¼ cups (8 oz) rice
½ cup (2 oz) grated Parmesan cheese
½ cup (2 oz) fine dry breadcrumbs

1. Brown 1 of the onions in half the butter, add the pigeons or spatchcocks, the livers, giblets, and mushrooms.
2. When they are all browned, add the tomato purée. Cook it for 2 to 3 minutes then add the wine and seasoning. Add half the stock and simmer for 1½ hours. If necessary, from time to time add more of the stock.
3. Cook the rice with the remaining onion, butter and remaining stock.
4. When it is almost cooked, add the cooking juice from the pigeons. Remove the pan from the heat and mix in the Parmesan.
5. Preheat the oven to 150°C (300°F/Gas 2).
6. Butter the bottom and sides of a round mould or cake tin 20 cm (8 in.) in diameter and sprinkle with half the breadcrumbs.
7. Put half the rice into the tin. Cut each bird into 4 pieces and put them on top of the rice. Cover with the remaining rice, sprinkle it with the rest of the breadcrumbs and dot with butter.
8. Place the tin in the preheated oven and cook for 1 to 1½ hours.
9. To serve, ease it carefully onto a serving platter.

Sfrappole
Carnival Twists

A delicious sweetmeat traditionally eaten during the Carnival period, these are also known as crespelli, chiacchiere or cenci.

Serves 6-8

500 g (1 lb) flour
¼ cup (2 oz) sugar
3 egg yolks
2 tablespoons brandy or rum
½ teaspoon grated lemon peel

60 g (2 oz) butter, melted
⅛ teaspoon salt
milk
oil for frying
icing (confectioners') sugar

1. In a bowl mix the flour, sugar, egg yolks, liquor, lemon peel, butter and salt.
2. Gradually, while stirring constantly, add enough milk to obtain a thick mixture.
3. Place it on a floured board and roll it out very thinly.
4. Cut the dough into rectangles 3 by 10 cm (1¼ by 4 in). In the centre of each, make an incision 2.5 cm (1 in) long and thread one end of the rectangle through it.
5. Preheat the oil in a saucepan and fry them to a light gold colour.
6. When they have cooled, dust them with plenty of icing sugar. Store them in an airtight jar to preserve freshness.

Torta di riso
Rice Cake

Serves 6

4 cups (1 litre) milk
⅓ cup (3 oz) sugar
1 teaspoon grated lemon peel
1¼ cups (8 oz) rice
¼ teaspoon salt

¾ cup (3 oz) blanched almonds,
  chopped
3-4 blanched bitter almonds, chopped
4 eggs, separated
¼ cup (1 oz) dry breadcrumbs

1. Preheat the oven to 150°C (300°F/Gas 2).
2. Heat the milk together with the sugar and lemon peel.
3. When it boils, add the rice and salt. Simmer.
4. When the rice has absorbed all the milk, remove from the heat and cool.
5. Add the almonds and the egg yolks to the rice mixture, stirring vigorously.
6. Beat the egg whites until stiff and fold them into the mixture.
7. Pour it into a buttered cake tin, sprinkle the top with the breadcrumbs and cook in the preheated oven for 40 minutes.

Pasticcio di maccheroni
Macaroni Pie

This unusual dessert, originally from Lazio, has a sweet pastry and a meat sauce.

Serves 4-6

315 g (10 oz) macaroni, cooked
½ portion of sauce diablo, Stage 1
  (see p.78)
2½ cups (10 oz) flour

155 g (5 oz) butter
⅓ cup (3 oz) sugar
1 egg
1 egg yolk

1. Preheat the oven to 190°C (375°F/Gas 5).
2. Mix the macaroni with the sauce and set aside.
3. Make a short pastry from the flour, butter, sugar, egg and egg yolk.
4. Line a soufflé dish with the short pastry, keeping some of it for the lid.
5. Fill the dish with the macaroni-sauce mixture, cover with the pastry lid and bake in the preheated oven for half an hour or until the pastry is golden-brown.

Amarelli o amaretti di Modena
Modena Macaroons

Makes 14-16 macaroons

¾ cup (4 oz) blanched almonds
1¼ cups (8 oz) caster (powdered)
  sugar

2-3 egg whites
2 tablespoons Kirsch

1. Preheat the oven to 180°C (350°F/Gas 4).
2. In a mortar, a mincer or food processor grind the almonds finely.
3. Place in a bowl, add 1 egg white, mix well and then add the sugar. Continue mixing and then add the second egg white and the Kirsch.
4. Form the dough into small biscuits and arrange them on a buttered baking tray, keeping some distance between them as they expand while baking.
5. Place them in the preheated oven and bake for 30 to 40 minutes.

The Marches

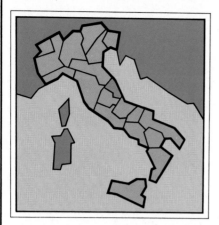

The people of the Marches are proud of their cooking and rightly so, for although it is not one of Italy's best known cuisines, it has a simple rustic quality that uses the excellent local produce to its best advantage.

When I was in Ancona I met Nicola Mazzera Morresi, who has recently written an impressive 450-page book on the cooking of the Marches.

She collected hundreds of regional recipes and the book is illustrated with colourful children's drawings.

The region's economy depends upon agriculture and fishing; there is very little industry. Wheat, cattle, sheep and vegetables all grow well here.

One of the region's most famous dishes is vincisgrassi. It is a rich version of lasagna, invented in 1799 by a chef in honour of Prince Alfred zu Windischgrätz, the Commander of the Austrian occupation forces. We have to assume that vincisgrassi was the chef's own spelling of Windischgrätz.

The olives of the Marches are particularly highly regarded, especially when they are stuffed, breadcrumbed and fried. Known as olive all'ascolana, they are exported to all parts of Italy.

On the coast, brodetto (fish stew, soup or chowder, depending upon where it is made) is the dish most often connected with the area. The people of the Marches proclaim that theirs is the most delicious, though almost all the coastal towns of the Marches have their own version and each one insists that its brodetto is the best. It is a mixture of many different types of fish, depending on the catch of the day. Some versions use saffron, some don't; some use white wine, some use tomato. The original version is thought to have been invented by the ancient Greeks.

Romanesque church in Portonovo near Ancona.

Brodetto alla anconetana

Ancona Fish Chowder

Serves 6

1 large onion, sliced
1 clove garlic, crushed
½ cup (4 fl oz) olive oil
1 tablespoon parsley, chopped
500 g (1 lb) tomatoes, peeled and
  chopped
2 tablespoons tomato purée
salt
freshly ground black pepper

⅛ teaspoon cayenne pepper
1 teaspoon white wine vinegar
1 kg (2 lb) 3-4 varieties of white-fleshed
  fish, cut into pieces
6 mussels
2 small squid, chopped
6 slices Italian bread, cut thick and
  toasted

1. Fry the onion and the garlic in the oil, add the parsley, tomatoes, tomato purée, salt, pepper, cayenne and vinegar. Cook for 3 minutes.
2. Add the seafood, bring to the boil and cook gently for 20 minutes. If necessary add some water. (The mussels will open during the cooking. Serve them in their shells.)
3. Place a slice of toasted bread in each soup plate and pour the soup over.

Pizza rustica

Country-Style Pizza

This pizza is in actual fact a pie made with pastry. A second layer of pastry in the form of a lid is placed on top of the pizza.

Serves 4

PASTRY:
2¾ cups (11 oz) flour
salt
125 g (4 oz) butter
water
FILLING:
2 tablespoons butter
2 tablespoons flour
1½-2 cups (12-16 fl oz) hot milk
2 egg yolks

¾ cup (3 oz) grated Parmesan cheese
90 g (3 oz) ricotta cheese
125 g (4 oz) Bel Paese cheese, diced
90 g (3 oz) prosciutto, chopped
90 g (3 oz) salami, chopped
2 eggs, hard-boiled and chopped
¼ cup (1½ oz) sultanas
salt
freshly ground black pepper

Pastry

1. Combine the flour, salt and butter and gently rub with the fingertips until it is the texture of fine breadcrumbs.
2. Stir in the water and mix until the dough comes away from the sides of the bowl. Transfer it to a floured board and knead vigorously. Place the dough in a buttered bowl and allow it to rest for half an hour.
3. Divide the dough into two parts, one slightly larger that the other.
4. Roll them into a 30 cm (12 in) and a 25 cm (10 in) round. Line the bottom and sides of a 25 cm (10 in) round pan with the large round.
5. Preheat the oven to 200°C (400°F/Gas 6).

Filling

1. Make a Béchamel sauce: Melt the butter, add the flour and gently cook for 5 minutes. Stir in the hot milk and cook for a further 5 minutes. When the Béchamel is cooked add the egg yolks (keep a little of the egg yolks for glazing the pizza lid).
2. Add the remaining ingredients and pour it into the pastry-lined dish.
3. Cover with the pastry lid. Press the edges to seal. Brush the lid with the remaining egg yolk and bake in the preheated oven for 30 minutes or until the lid is golden brown.

Vincisgrassi
Rich Lasagna

An elaborate dish created in 1799 in honour of Prince Windischgrätz of Austria.

Serves 4

6 sheets ready-made lasagna
water
salt
2 calves' brains
2 calves' sweetbreads
3 tablespoons lard or bacon fat
1 onion, chopped
1 carrot, chopped
250 g (8 oz) chicken giblets
1 cup (8 fl oz) dry white wine
1 tablespoon concentrated tomato
  purée

½ cup (4 fl oz) chicken stock or water
salt
pepper
BÉCHAMEL SAUCE:
2 tablespoons butter
2 tablespoons flour
1 cup (8 fl oz) hot milk
½ teaspoon nutmeg
1 cup (4 oz) grated Parmesan cheese
melted butter

1. Preheat the oven to 190°C (375°F/Gas 5).
2. Cook the lasagna in boiling salted water for 5 to 8 minutes.
3. In another pan of boiling salted water blanch the brains and the sweetbreads for 5 minutes.
4. Melt the fat and sauté the onion and carrot, add the chopped chicken giblets and the wine.
5. Cook until the wine has almost evaporated, add the tomato purée and the chicken stock or water.
6. Season, cover and cook gently for 1 hour. Stir occasionally.
7. Fifteen minutes befor it is cooked, add the diced brains and sweetbreads.
8. Make a Béchamel sauce by melting the butter in a pan over a low heat. Add the flour and cook until golden.
9. Stir in the hot milk, and cook on a low heat stirring constantly for 5 minutes. Season, add the nutmeg and continue cooking for a further 10 minutes.
10. Grease an ovenproof dish and arrange alternate layers of pasta, Béchamel sauce, cheese and the meat sauce, finishing up with a layer of Béchamel.
11. Bake in the preheated oven for 30 to 40 minutes. Pour some melted butter on top and serve piping hot sprinkled with cheese.

Cavolfiore fritto
Fried Cauliflower in Batter

Serves 4

1 kg (2 lb) cauliflower in one piece
¾ cup (3 oz) flour
1 egg
dry white wine

1 teaspoon aniseed liqueur (optional)
salt
freshly ground black pepper
oil for frying

1. Boil the cauliflower, covered, in salted water for 10 to 15 minutes until it is tender but still firm.
2. To make the batter, mix the flour, egg and sufficient wine to make a batter which will be thick enough to cling to the cauliflower. Add the aniseed liqueur and season to taste.
3. Drain the cauliflower and when cool divide it into flowerets.
4. Heat the oil.
5. Dip the flowerets in the batter and fry them in the oil until light brown. Sprinkle with salt and freshly ground black pepper and serve the cauliflower hot.

Stoccafisso all'anconitana

Dried Cod (Stockfish) with Potatoes

This is a speciality of the Passetto restaurant in Ancona.

Serves 4

750 g (1½ lb) dried cod
½ cup (4 fl oz) olive oil
2 onions, chopped
2 tablespoons finely chopped fresh
  marjoram
2 carrots, chopped
2 celery stalks, chopped
¼ cup chopped parsley

1 clove garlic, crushed
salt
freshly ground pepper
2-3 fillets anchovy, chopped (optional)
2 tomatoes, peeled and sliced
½ cup (4 fl oz) dry white wine
4 potatoes, each cut into four

1. Soak the fish in a large quantity of cold water, preferably in the refrigerator, for between 3 to 8 days. The water should be changed frequently. The length of soaking depends on how dry the fish was in the first place. Finally it should regain the softness it had before it had been dried.
2. Drain and dry the fish, remove any bones and cut into pieces approximately 10 cm (4 in) long.
3. In a heavy-bottomed casserole, heat half the oil and sauté the onions until golden brown. Add the marjoram, carrots, celery, parsley and garlic together with the salt and large quantities of freshly ground pepper. If desired, also add the finely chopped anchovy.
4. Sauté this mixture for a few moments and then add the tomatoes. Cook for a further 5 minutes, set aside.
5. The original recipe calls for the fish to be cooked in an earthenware pot. If this is not available, a cast-iron heavy-bottomed casserole can be used. During the cooking the fish may stick to the bottom and if possible a rack should be placed on the bottom of the pot. When arranging the fish in the pot, place it in layers with the skin side facing upwards.
6. Cover the fish with the above prepared sauce. Pour the remaining oil over the top and add the wine. Cover the pan.
7. Cook the fish on a slow heat for approximately 2 hours, shaking the pot from time to time.
8. Approximately 1 hour before the fish is cooked place the potatoes on top of it.
9. When the cooking is completed, remove the potatoes and skim off any surplus fat from the top of the saucepan. Cover again and allow it to stand for approximately 15 minutes.
10. Serve the fish together with the potatoes from the dish in which it was cooked.

Passetto, Ancona

High above the cliffs of Passetto, Ancona's beach, is the Passetto restaurant. It overlooks a very pretty part of what is known as the Riviera del Conero, a stretch of sparkling scenic Adriatic coast. One of the best-known local antipasti is olive ascolane, stuffed olives, in which the stone has been removed and replaced with a mixture of three to four types of finely minced meats and herbs. At Passetto they serve a very fine vincisgrassi, an elaborate type of lasagna. Other dishes such as stoccofisco (dried cod) are regional specialities, and the finest dish I tried was suppa di balleni, made from a mussel-type mollusc which lives in a stone. They are very expensive to catch as the stone has to be broken up to extract the creature. The Molluscs are then steamed with tomatoes, olive oil, white wine and parsley. The result is most delectable. The most typical local wine is Verdicchio del Castelli de Jesi, a very dry white wine which goes so well with the local seafood.

Above: *dried cod with potatoes (see p.94); vincisgrassi (see p.93).*

Calamaretti delle Marche

Squid in Wine and Chilli Sauce

Serves 6

1 clove garlic, crushed
½ cup (4 fl oz) olive oil
1.5 kg (3 lb) squid, cleaned and
  chopped
salt

1 small piece hot chilli, finely chopped
  (or pinch of cayenne pepper)
1 cup (8 fl oz) dry white wine
¾ cup (6 fl oz) fish stock
4 sprigs parsley, finely chopped

1. Fry the garlic in the olive oil and then add the squid, salt and chilli or cayenne pepper to taste.
2. Cook the squid for approximately 10 minutes, add the wine and cook for a further 10 minutes. Add the stock and cover the dish.
3. Simmer for approximately 30 minutes until the squid is tender. Sprinkle with parsley.
4. This dish may be served with boiled rice or a pasta dish.

Riso e fagioli

Rice and Beans

Serves 4

2 cups (12 oz) fresh, shelled broad
  beans (or dried white beans, soaked
  overnight in water and drained)
2 tablespoons olive oil
1 onion, chopped
1 stalk celery, chopped

2 large tomatoes, peeled and chopped
salt
cayenne pepper
½ cup (3 oz) rice
½ cup (2 oz) grated Romano cheese

1. Simmer the beans in salted water until cooked and tender. (Approximately 15 minutes for fresh beans, 40 to 45 minutes for soaked dried beans.)
2. In a saucepan heat the oil and sauté the onion and the celery until brown.
3. Add the tomatoes and season.
4. Add the beans with their cooking water and then the rice.
5. Cook for 20 minutes. The result should be a thick soup.
6. Serve with the grated cheese.

Agnello con olive

Lamb with Olives

Serves 4

6 tablespoons olive oil
4 lamb leg steaks, about 1.5 cm (½ in)
  thick
salt
freshly ground black pepper
1 cup (5 oz) black olives, pitted and
  chopped

½ teaspoon dried oregano
3 tablespoons green peppers
  (capsicums), chopped
juice ½ lemon

1. In a frying pan heat the oil and brown the steaks on both sides. Drain off some of the fat and season.
2. Add the olives, sprinkle with the oregano, add the green peppers and lemon juice and simmer for 4 to 5 minutes before serving.

Abbacchio al forno
Roast Baby Lamb

Traditionally, this should be spit-roasted, however it is quite delicious when baked in the oven.

Serves 4-6

1 leg of baby lamb (allow 315 g (10 oz)
   gross weight per person)
2 cloves garlic, cut into slivers
2 sprigs fresh rosemary

2-3 tablespoons olive oil
salt
freshly ground black pepper
1 cup (8 fl oz) dry white wine

1. Preheat the oven to 190°C (375°F/Gas 5).
2. With a sharp knife cut small pockets in the leg and insert a sliver of garlic and some rosemary in each.
3. Brush the leg with oil and sprinkle it with salt and pepper.
4. Place the leg in an oiled roasting pan and cook in the preheated oven for 1 hour. Do not overcook; the meat should be slightly pink.
5. Pour the wine into the pan about half an hour before the roasting is completed. Check after 15 minutes and if necessary, add some water.
6. When the leg is cooked, remove it to a carving board. Remove any excess fat from the cooking juices and boil rapidly to reduce it. Season and pour it over the carved slices of lamb.

Pollo alla maceratese
Poached Chicken with Egg and Lemon Sauce

Serves 4

1.5 kg (3 lb) chicken
125 g (4 oz) chicken giblets, chopped
salt
½ cup (4 fl oz) olive oil

2 cups (16 fl oz) chicken stock
2 egg yolks
juice 1 lemon
freshly ground black pepper

1. In a deep heavy-bottomed casserole, brown the chicken and the giblets, which have been sprinkled with salt, in the olive oil.
2. Add the stock, cover the casserole and simmer it over a low heat for approximately 1 hour.
3. When the chicken has cooked, remove it from the casserole and keep it warm. Boil the stock until it reduces slightly.
4. Mix the egg yolks with the lemon juice, salt and pepper, and add to the cooking juices in the casserole.
5. Cook over a low heat for 1 to 2 minutes, stirring constantly, making sure that it does not boil and curdle.
6. To serve, carve the chicken into pieces, arrange them on a serving platter and pour the sauce over them.

Lombardy

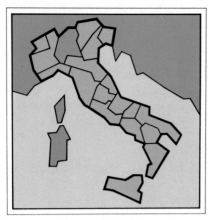

The cooking of Lombardy and that of its capital, Milan, are almost interchangeable.

One of Lombardy's most important products is cattle: this has two effects on the cuisine. The first is that beef is the favourite meat in the province, unlike most of Italy, where veal and pork far outstrip beef in popularity. The second is that because of its huge milk supply, the cooking of Lombardy is done almost entirely in butter rather than the olive oil we've come to expect in Italian cooking. It also means that cheese is one of Lombardy's most famous products.

Gorgonzola, probably the most well-known cheese from the region has an interesting history: each year, herds of cattle were moved from the summer pastures in the mountains to the plains and they stopped to rest in a little town about ten miles from Milan: Gorgonzola. As a result, every year Gorgonzola had much too much milk. So they turned it into cheese and aged it in the caves of the Valsassina. Bel Paese is also made in Lombardy as is grana, mascarpone and taleggio.

Another of the famous products of Lombardy is rice from the Po valley. Risotto alla milanese is known all over the world; usually it is served as a course on its own, except when served with that other delicious Milanese dish, ossobuco. Minestrone alla milanese is different from minestrone from other regions in that it uses rice instead of pasta.

Then there's costoletta alla milanese which is said to have been the forerunner to wiener schnitzel; and polenta. Polenta is very popular in Lombardy and has been for many centuries. It is a simple mixture of cornmeal and water. It can be eaten hot and creamy, or it can be allowed to cool and harden, after which it is cut into cubes and fried in butter or oil, or toasted or baked, or made into polenta pie.

Lesso misto, which is a version of the famous bollito misto is boiled meats, usually served with salsa verde (green sauce) or mostarda (mustard fruits), a famous product from Cremona in the south of Lombardy.

Panettone is one of Lombardy's most famous foods. It is a cake-like bread containing raisins and candied peel, similar to the German Kugelhof. It keeps fresh a long time and is found in Italian cake shops all over the world, especially at Christmas time.

But these are only a few of the most famous dishes in Lombardy. It's an extremely rich area, both in its natural produce and its cuisine.

Ville D'Este on Lake Como.

Zuppa di trippa
Tripe Soup

This recipe comes from Crott di Cameli in Dongo, Lake Como.

Serves 4

1 kg (2 lb) tripe, cut into small strips
2 pigs' trotters
4 cups (1 litre) beef stock
90 g (3 oz) salt pork, cut into small
  chunks
1 large onion, roughly chopped
1 carrot, finely chopped

1 clove garlic, crushed
2 tablespoons olive oil
1 cup Bolognese meat sauce
  (see page 86)
salt
pepper
grated Parmesan cheese for garnish

1. In a large saucepan combine the tripe, pigs' trotters, beef stock and the salted pork.
2. Lightly fry the onion, carrot and garlic in the olive oil and add them to the saucepan. Simmer for 1½ hours.
3. Add the Bolognese meat sauce and cook for a further 30 minutes.
4. If necessary, season and serve hot, sprinkled with Parmesan cheese.

Minestrone alla milanese
Milanese Thick Vegetable Soup

Milanese minestrone is distinguished by the use of rice, while those in other parts of Italy use pasta.

Serves 4

30 g (1 oz) butter
4 slices bacon, finely chopped
1 cup chopped parsley
1 clove garlic, crushed
1 stalk celery, chopped
2 potatoes, diced
2 carrots, chopped
2 zucchinis (courgettes), sliced
125 g (4 oz) green beans, cut into
  1.5 cm (½ in) long pieces

1 cup (6 oz) dried beans, previously
  soaked for 12 hours
3 tomatoes, peeled and chopped
salt
freshly ground black pepper
110 g (3½ oz) cabbage, coarsely
  chopped
1 cup (6 oz) rice
4 tablespoons Parmesan cheese
  (optional)

1. Melt the butter in a saucepan, add the bacon, parsley, garlic and celery. Sauté for 5 minutes.
2. Add the potatoes, carrots, zucchinis, green and dried beans and tomatoes. Season and cover with water. Cover the pan and simmer for half an hour.
3. Add the cabbage and the rice and simmer for a further half hour. Make sure the rice is not overcooked.
4. Serve it, if desired, with a sprinkling of Parmesan.

Zuppa pavese
Soup with Poached Eggs

Serves 4

1 loaf French bread
2 tablespoons butter
¼ cup (2 fl oz) olive oil
4 cups (1 litre) chicken or beef
  consommé

4 eggs
4 tablespoons grated Parmesan cheese

1. Cut the bread into 2.5 cm (1 in) slices and fry them in the butter-oil mixture.
2. Boil the consommé, turn down the heat and while simmering it lightly, break the eggs one at a time, into a saucer and gently slide them into the consommé.
3. When the eggs are poached, place the toasted bread in the soup bowl, place the egg on top of the toast, gently pour the consommé over and sprinkle with Parmesan.

Salsa verde alla milanese
Milanese Parsley Sauce

A food processor is ideal for the preparation of this sauce.

Serves 6

½ clove garlic, crushed
2 tablespoons fine dry breadcrumbs
1 egg, hard-boiled and finely chopped
2 anchovy fillets, finely chopped
½ tablespoon finely chopped capers

4 sprigs parsley, finely chopped
salt
freshly ground black pepper
olive oil

1. Place all the ingredients except the olive oil into the processor and purée for approximately 10 to 15 seconds.
2. While processing, gradually add the oil. Anything between ¾ to 1 cup may be required.
3. If you do not have a food processor, pound all the ingredients, except the oil, with a mortar and pestle. Add the oil a little at a time, as if you were making mayonnaise.
4. The sauce should be left to stand for 2 to 4 hours before serving. Traditionally it is served with a bulito misti, the traditional Milanese boiled meat dish.

Polenta
Polenta is of Etruscan origin and it was passed on to the Romans. It is most popular in northern Italy where the Etruscan influence on cooking is still felt.

Serves 6

6 cups (1.5 litres) water or half water
  and half milk
1 teaspoon salt

2¾ cups (11 oz) polenta (yellow corn
  meal)

1. Boil the water or water-milk mixture and add the salt.
2. Lower the heat and gradually add the polenta, stirring constantly to prevent it from sticking to the bottom and forming lumps.
3. Cook gently for 45 minutes, stirring occasionally.
4. When cooked, it can be either poured into a serving platter and eaten immediately, or it can be poured onto a baking tray, cooled and then cut into squares, lozenges or triangles and fried in butter until crisp.

Risotto alla milanese
Risotto with Beef Marrow and White Wine

There are several versions of risotta alla milanese: cooked with chicken stock and flavoured with saffron; with butter and Parmesan cheese added at the end of the cooking. Another version is cooked with beef marrow and white wine, and a third is flavoured with Marsala wine. In each case saffron is used as a flavouring.

Serves 6

2 tablespoons butter
3 tablespoons onions, chopped
60 g (2 oz) beef marrow
500 g (1 lb) rice
¾ cup (6 fl oz) dry white wine

6 cups (1.5 litres) chicken stock
½ teaspoon powdered saffron
2 tablespoons butter
1 cup (4 oz) grated Parmesan cheese

1. In a saucepan, melt the butter and lightly fry the onions. Add the chopped beef marrow, stir in the rice and make sure it is well coated with butter.
2. Pour in the wine and cook it over a low heat until it has almost evaporated. Start adding the stock one cup at a time. When the stock becomes absorbed, add more.
3. The cooking will take approximately 20 to 30 minutes. Towards the end, stir continuously with a fork.
4. When the rice is cooked, add the saffron (first diluted in a little stock or water).
5. Before serving, mix in the butter and 2 tablespoons of the Parmesan. Serve the remaining Parmesan at the table.

Asparagi alla milanese
Asparagus Milanese Style

Serves 4

750 g (1½ lb) asparagus
water
4 eggs
125 g (4 oz) butter

salt
freshly ground black pepper
½ cup (2 oz) Parmesan cheese

1. Tie the asparagus into 4 equal bundles. If you don't have an asparagus steamer, use your tallest saucepan. Stand the bundles vertically and if they protrude above the rim, cover the saucepan with another of the same diameter, turned upside-down.
2. Pour in about 5 cm (2 in) of water and boil for 15 minutes.
3. In the meantime, fry the eggs in the butter.
4. Lift the eggs out onto the dinner plates and place the asparagus next to them. Pour the butter over the asparagus and sprinkle it all with Parmesan.

Oasi della Pace, Rivanazzano (near Pavia)
The Oasis of Peace is a convent run by the Family of Sisters of Saint Rosario, Apostle of Work. I don't know the origin of it all but I presume that some enterprising ladies of the Order who were providing food for the aged guests holidaying in the convent decided to cater for the general public. And what a wise decision. The Mother Superior, Sister Maria Anna Corelli, has gathered a group of very talented sisters who do the catering. Sister Teresa acts as 'chef' and she is supported in her efforts by several others who are in charge of the various preparations. Sister Eda, for example, is a Venetian and prepares their famous antipasti, while Sister Imigina from Cremona is responsible for all their delicious desserts. The result is quite extraordinary. People come from far and wide to taste the result of their culinary endeavours.

Above: *clockwise from bottom left: smoked salmon in aspic; St. Honoré cake; sandwiches Margherita; fresh fruit tart; fettucine in wine sauce; spring roll (see p.104).*

Rotolo alla primavera

Spring Roll

This is a speciality of the Oasi della Pace in Rivanazzano.

Serves 12

8 egg yolks
8 egg whites, beaten stiff
1 teaspoon salt

1¼ cups (5 oz) flour
2 cups (16 fl oz) mayonnaise
500 g (1 lb) cooked ham, sliced

1. Preheat the oven to 150°C (300°F/Gas 2).
2. Beat the egg yolks with a little salt.
3. To the egg yolks, add alternately, a spoonful at a time, the flour sifted with the remaining salt, and the beaten egg white. Combine them carefully.
4. On an oven dish, spread out some oiled aluminium foil and pour the mixture evenly over it.
5. Place the dish in the preheated oven and cook for 8 to 12 minutes.
6. Turn the baked pasta onto a moist napkin, remove the aluminium and allow to cool.
7. Spread the mayonnaise evenly all over the pasta square and cover it with the slices of ham.
8. Roll the pasta up tightly and wrap it in the same napkin.
9. To serve, cut the pasta into slices and arrange them on a serving platter.

Sedano alla milanese

Gratin of Celery

This recipe comes from the Crotto del Misto in Lezzeno. It is a delightful old inn on the shores of the beautiful Lake Como. Its food is remarkable, especially the fish from the lake and the veal dishes.
Crotto del Misto has an extensive cellar with a wide range of fine and aged wine.
You can reach Lezzeno by road but the ninety minute journey by ferry is a wonderful experience. The villages along the lake, painted in subtle pastel colours hang on the steep mountain slopes. And elegant villas for which the lake is famous dot the shoreline.

Serves 4

2 bunches celery
stock or water
salt
cayenne pepper
½ cup (2 oz) grated Parmesan cheese

BÉCHAMEL SAUCE:
2 tablespoons butter
2 tablespoons flour
2½ cups (20 fl oz) hot milk
salt
freshly ground black pepper
¼ teaspoon nutmeg

1. Preheat the oven to 200°C (400°F/Gas 6).
2. Cut the stalk end of the celery bunches so that they are about 15 cm (6 in) long. Leave the stalks attached at the roots. Cut each bunch lengthwise in half and wash thoroughly.
3. Place the 4 halves in a shallow pan, and pour in enough stock or water to cover. Season with salt and cayenne.
4. Cover the dish and simmer the celery for 10 minutes on a low heat.
5. To make the Béchamel sauce: Melt the butter, add the flour and cook it for 4 to 5 minutes without browning it. Add the milk, stirring constantly. Cook for 15 minutes, stirring from time to time. Season and add the nutmeg.
6. Transfer the celery to an ovenproof dish, pour the Béchamel over the celery and sprinkle it with half the Parmesan cheese.
7. Place the dish in the preheated oven and bake for about 15 to 20 minutes or until the top is brown.
8. Serve it sprinkled with the rest of the Parmesan.

Spinaci alla parmigiana
Parmesan Spinach

Serves 6

1 kg (2 lb) spinach, washed and
   chopped
100 g (3½ oz) butter
salt

freshly ground black pepper
½ teaspoon nutmeg
½ cup (2 oz) grated Parmesan cheese

In a saucepan, combine the spinach and the butter. Cook for 8 to 10 minutes, add the salt, pepper and nutmeg. Mix in the Parmesan and serve very hot.

Broccoli o cavolfiori alla milanese
Broccoli or Cauliflower, Milanese Style

Serves 4

1 cauliflower or broccoli weighing
   1-1.25 kg (2-2½ lb)
water
salt
¼ cup (1 oz) flour
2 eggs, whisked with a little water

1 cup (4 oz) grated Parmesan cheese
1 cup (4 oz) fine dry breadcrumbs
salt
freshly ground black pepper
250 g (8 oz) butter

1. Break up the cauliflower or the broccoli into bite-size flowerets and boil them in salted water for 5 minutes.
2. Drain them, dust them with flour, dip them in the egg mixture, then in the cheese, again in the egg and finally in the breadcrumbs. Season.
3. Fry them in the butter until the breadcrumbs are golden-brown.

Torta di cipolle
Onion Pie

This recipe comes from the Chalet Della Certosa in Pavia.

Makes 23 cm (9 in.) pie

600 g (1 lb 3 oz) onions, finely
   chopped
90 g (3 oz) smoked fat bacon,
   chopped
3 tablespoons oil
4 eggs

2 egg whites, beaten stiff
salt
freshly ground pepper
puff pastry, sufficient to make 2 crusts
   for a 23 cm (9 in) pie dish
egg wash to glaze

1. Preheat the oven to 190°C (375°F/Gas 5).
2. Place the onions, bacon and oil in a frying pan and sauté them until the onions are soft.
3. Remove from the heat and incorporate 4 eggs, lightly beaten, and the egg whites, together with some salt and pepper.
4. Grease the pie dish and line it with the puff pastry. Pour the mixture into the pie and cover with a pastry lid. Brush the lid with egg wash.
5. Bake the pie in the preheated oven for 45 minutes. It may be served either hot or cold.

Filetti di tacchino

Breasts of Turkey

This dish can also be prepared with chicken fillets.

Serves 4

410-500 g (13-16 oz) breast of turkey,
  cut into thin slices
salt
freshly ground black pepper
¼ cup (1 oz) flour

125 g (4 oz) butter
4 slices prosciutto or cooked ham
6-8 button mushrooms, finely chopped
½ cup (2 oz) grated Parmesan cheese
½ cup (4 fl oz) chicken or turkey stock

1. Season the turkey fillets, dust them with flour and lightly brown them in the butter.
2. Place a slice of ham on each slice of turkey and cover them with the mushrooms which have been previously sautéed in butter. Sprinkle them with the cheese and moisten them with the stock.
3. Place them in a pan, cover and gently simmer for 5 to 8 minutes. If the cooking juice has evaporated too much add more stock.
4. Serve the fillets masked with the cooking juice which should have thickened to a cream-like consistency.

Tacchina ripiena alla lombarda

Lombardian Stuffed Turkey

Serves 8-10

1 turkey, about 4 kg (8 lb)
salt
freshly ground black pepper
3 tablespoons butter mixed with a little
  finely chopped sage and rosemary
4 slices prosciutto
4 cups (1 litre) dry white wine
STUFFING:
250 g (8 oz) veal, minced
125 g (4 oz) lean pork, minced
125 g (4 oz) beef, minced
220 g (7 oz) chipolata sausage,
  chopped

3 eggs
4 tablespoons grated Parmesan cheese
¼ teaspoon nutmeg
125 g (4 oz) prunes, stoned and
  chopped
2-3 cooking apples, peeled and diced
15 chestnuts, boiled, peeled and
  mashed
2 slices bacon, coarsely chopped
salt
freshly ground black pepper

1. Preheat the oven to 180°C (350°F/Gas 4).
2. Combine all the stuffing ingredients and place them in the cavity of the turkey. Sew up the opening.
3. Place the turkey in a large roasting pan, dot with the herb butter and cover the bird with prosciutto. Add 2 cups of the wine to the pan and place the turkey in the preheated oven.
4. Roast it for 2½ hours, remove the prosciutto and return the turkey to the oven for a further 20 to 30 minutes to brown the skin.
5. Remove the turkey from the roasting pan. Skim off the excess fat. Add the remaining wine, bring to the boil, season and serve separately in a sauce boat.

Chalet della Certosa, Certosa di Pavia
The restaurant is located just outside the gates of the famous Carthusian Monastery the Certosa di Pavia. Its owner, Piero Bolfo, has always been interested in furthering the cause of regional foods and at the Chalet he serves a very impressive array of regional and local dishes. Rabbit alla pavese, chicken with mint, and two types of savoury tarts, one made with polenta and the other with onions, were outstanding and unusual dishes. The monks at the monastery offer some very good home-made liqueurs and wines, which I presume come from their own vineyards.

Above: *onion pie (see p.105).*

Scaloppine alla milanese
Small Escalopes of Veal, Milanese Style

Scaloppine are small squares of veal, sliced very thinly and lightly cooked in butter. There are many ways of garnishing them and they form an important part of Lombardy cooking, especially that of Milan.

Serves 4

**500 g (1 lb) thin veal escalopes cut
from the fillet or the inside of the
leg
salt**

**freshly ground black pepper
juice 1½-2 lemons
¼ cup (1 oz) flour
60-125 g (2-4 oz) butter**

1. Cut the escalopes thinly into 7.5 cm (3 in) squares, each weighing approximately 30 g (1 oz). Allow 3 to 4 slices per person.
2. Beat them flat, season them and sprinkle with lemon juice. Dust them with flour.
3. Melt the butter in a frying pan and brown the pieces on both sides.

Variations:

Scaloppine con i capperi
Scaloppine with Capers

Fry 1 chopped onion in the butter, add 2 tablespoons of capers and then cook the meat as above.

Scaloppine con olio e lemone
Scaloppine with Olive Oil and Lemon

Before cooking, marinate the veal in a mixture of ¼ cup (2 fl. oz.) olive oil and the juice of 2 lemons. Pour the marinade into the pan and cook the veal in it.

Scaloppine al pomodore
Scaloppine with Tomatoes

Fry 1 chopped onion in the butter with 2 chopped peeled tomatoes and add then cook the veal as above.

Scaloppine in salsa picanta
Scaloppine in Piquant Sauce

Heat ½ cup (4 fl. oz.) veal stock and 2 tablespoons each of chopped mixed pickles, pickled peppers and mushrooms in the pan before the meat is cooked.

Scaloppine al Marsala
Scaloppine in Marsala

Add 2 tablespoons of Marsala to the meat in the pan and simmer for 2 minutes.

Scaloppine al fromaggio
Scaloppine with cheese

Add ½ cup (4 fl oz) white wine to the pan, cover each slice of meat with a slice of cheese, cover and simmer for 2 to 3 minutes until the cheese melts.

Vitello tonnato
Cold Braised Veal with Tuna Mayonnaise

This is a delicious and very popular Italian summer dish which both Lombardy and Piedmont claim as their own.
Other cuts of veal such as boned leg may be used, but shoulder meat produces the best texture.

1.75 kg (3¼ lb) rolled shoulder of veal
6 anchovy fillets, cut into 2.5 cm (1 in) lengths
2 cloves garlic, cut into slivers
2 cups (16 fl oz) dry white wine
water
2 onions, roughly chopped
2 carrots, sliced
3 bay leaves
12 peppercorns
6 sprigs parsley
1 clove
TUNA MAYONNAISE:
2 eggs
½ cup (4 fl oz) olive oil

4 anchovy fillets
1 tin (approx. 100 g) tuna in brine, drained
2 tablespoons capers
juice 1 lemon
½ cup (4 fl oz) sour cream
salt
pepper
GARNISH:
12 lemon slices, cut in half
3 sprigs parsley, finely chopped
2 tablespoons capers
12 black olives

1. With a sharp knife, make pockets in the rolled shoulder and insert a piece of anchovy and a sliver of garlic in each.
2. Place the meat in an oval casserole and add the wine, enough water to cover the meat, onions, carrots, celery, bay leaves, peppercorns, parsley and clove.
3. Cover the casserole and slowly bring it to the boil. Remove any scum that gathers on the surface. Simmer the meat on a low heat for 1¼ hours.
4. Allow the meat to cool in the liquid.

Mayonnaise
1. Place the eggs in a food processor and blend for 10 to 15 seconds.
2. Gradually, drop by drop, add the oil so that the mayonnaise emulsifies.
3. Add the anchovy, tuna and capers and process long enough to purée them.
4. Add the lemon juice, sour cream, salt and pepper and process for 2 to 3 seconds.
5. Taste, and if necessary season or add more lemon juice.

Note: If you don't have a food processor, make the mayonnaise in the usual way, then add the mashed tuna, anchovy and capers. Stir in the remaining ingredients with a wire whisk.

To Serve
1. Cut the cooled meat into thin slices and arrange them on a platter.
2. Mask the meat generously with the mayonnaise and serve the remainder of it in a sauce boat.
3. Garnish the platter with lemon slices, sprinkle it with the parsley and arrange the capers and black olives to form a decorative pattern.
4. The dish should be served cold accompanied by a fresh salad.

Ossobuco alla milanese

Veal Shanks Milan Style

This recipe comes from Villa d'Este on Lake Como.

Serves 6

4 tablespoons butter
2 large onions, chopped
1 carrot, chopped
1 stalk celery, chopped
1 clove garlic, crushed
6-8 pieces meaty veal shanks, cut into
    5 cm (2 in) slices
salt
freshly ground black pepper
½ cup (2 oz) flour
½ cup (4 fl oz) olive oil

1¼ cups (10 fl oz) dry white wine
¾ cup (6 fl oz) beef or chicken stock
1 teaspoon mixed dried herbs
750 g (1½ lb) canned whole tomatoes,
    chopped
½ cup chopped parsley
3 bay leaves
GREMOLATA:
1 clove garlic, crushed
3 teaspoons grated lemon peel
3 tablespoons finely chopped parsley

1. Preheat the oven to 180°C (350°F/Gas 4).
2. In a large frying pan, melt the butter and sauté the onions, carrots, celery and garlic. Continue cooking for 10 minutes until the vegetables have lightly browned.
3. Season the meat and dust the pieces with flour. In another large frying pan, heat the oil and fry the meat until it is brown all over.
4. Place the pieces of meat side by side in a casserole and cover with the vegetables.
5. Pour the wine into the frying pan in which the meat was cooked, add the stock, herbs, tomatoes, parsley and bay leaves. Bring to the boil, reduce slightly and then pour it over the meat. The liquid should come half way up the side of the meat. If necessary, add more stock.
6. Bring the casserole to the boil on top of the oven, cover and place it into the preheated oven. Cook for 1½ hours.
7. Serve the pieces of meat on individual plates and pour the sauce over the meat, sprinkled with some gremolata.

GREMOLATA
Mix the garlic, lemon peel and chopped parsley together.

Costolette alla milanese

Milanese Veal Cutlets

It is said that wiener schnitzel developed from the costeletta. The main difference is that the schnitzel is cut from the fillet or leg and the costoletta is a loin chop with the bone left on.

Serves 6

6 veal loin chops
salt
freshly ground black pepper
¼ cup (1 oz) flour
1 egg, whisked with a little water

½ cup (2 oz) fine dry breadcrumbs
125 g (4 oz) butter, clarified
6 lemon wedges
6 sprigs parsley

1. Cut off any fat or gristle from the chops and flatten them with a meat hammer or rolling pin. Season.
2. Dust the chops with flour, dip them in the egg-water mixture and generously coat them with the breadcrumbs.
3. Fry the chops in hot clarified butter over a medium heat for 8 to 10 minutes.
4. Serve them garnished with the lemon wedges and sprigs of parsley.

Villa d'Este, Lake Como

Villa d'Este justifiably enjoys the reputation of being one of the world's most luxurious hotels. Its setting on the shores of the beautiful Lake Como is breathtaking. It has always served good food but in recent years, under the direction of its Executive Chef, Luciano Parolari, it has gained for itself a name among gourmets. I went there to add to my collection of Lombardy dishes and in this respect I struck some problems. Villa d'Este, because of its international clientele does not specialise in regional food, but presents dishes of more national or international character. However, at the Villa d'Este nothing presents a problem. With the inspiration of Giovanna Salvatore, the kinetic public relations lady, Luciano soon produced an array of Lombardy dishes: the inevitable ossobuco, costoletta alla milanese, and Gorgonzola di Como, a delicious local cheese. Food eaten in pleasant surroundings improves greatly. The meal at the Villa d'Este was a feast!

Above: *Clockwise from bottom left: ossobuco (see p.110); veal cutlets (see p.110); bresaola (cured beef); crespelle in cheese sauce.*

111

Scaloppe farcite
Stuffed Veal Escalopes

Serves 4

410 g (13 oz) escalope of veal, cut into
  8 thin slices
salt
4 tablespoons butter
freshly ground black pepper

4 tablespoons finely diced mushrooms
4 tablespoons grated Parmesan cheese
4 slices leg ham, chopped
4 slices Gruyère cheese
1 cup (8 fl oz) beef stock

1. Season the thin slices of veal (2 per person) and lightly sauté them in half the butter. Remove the veal from the pan and set aside.
2. Lightly sauté the mushrooms in the same pan and season them, add the ham and the grated Parmesan. Mix well together but do not cook.
3. Make a sandwich with 2 slices of veal on the outside and the mushroom, ham and cheese mixture on the inside. Press the edges of the veal together and fasten with toothpicks.
4. Sauté the veal in the remaining butter for a few minutes only, place a slice of Gruyère on top of the veal, add the stock to the pan, cover and cook gently for 2 to 3 minutes.
5. To serve, pour the cooking juice over the veal.

Polpettone
Italian Meat Loaf

As with the polpette there are many ways of varying the preparation of the polpettone.

Serves 8

1 kg (2 lb) raw meat, minced (beef,
  pork, veal or a mixture)
4 eggs
2 cloves garlic, crushed
½ cup chopped parsley
salt
freshly ground black pepper

STUFFING:
2 eggs, hard-boiled and chopped
60 g (2 oz) cooked ham, chopped
60 g (2 oz) provolone or Gruyère
  cheese, chopped
salt
freshly ground black pepper

1. Preheat the oven to 150°C (300°F/Gas 2).
2. In a bowl mix the meat, eggs, garlic, parsley, salt and pepper.
3. Spread the mixture on a board.
4. In another bowl, mix together the stuffing ingredients.
5. Spread the stuffing in the centre of the meat, leaving a border all around of 2.5 cm (1 in).
6. Roll the meat into a loaf and place it on a buttered baking tray, or pack half the meat into a terrine, spread out the stuffing and cover with the rest of the meat.
7. Place the meat in the preheated oven and cook for 1½ hours.
8. Polpettone may be eaten either hot or cold.

The following are some of the variations prepared in Lombardy. Prepare as above, using the same proportions.

Polpettone di cotecchino: with veal or pork and cotecchino sausage.
Polpettone di fegato: with beef, beef liver and ham.
Polpettone di rognone: with veal, veal kidney, raw ham, sage and rosemary.
Polpettone con gli spinacci: with spinach, raw ham, egg, sage and rosemary.
Polpettone tritato arrosto: with beef, pork, veal, egg, sage and rosemary.
Polpettone tritato a lesso: with beef and mortadella sausage.

Polpette
Italian Meat Balls or Rissoles

Polpette can be made with raw beef, veal, pork, liver or cooked meat. The variations are endless.

Serves 6

500 g (1 lb) raw or cooked minced meat
1 egg
2 cloves garlic, crushed
1 thick slice of bread
1 cup (8 fl oz) milk
¼ cup chopped parsley

salt
freshly ground black pepper
¼ teaspoon nutmeg
¼ teaspoon grated lemon peel
¼ cup (1 oz) flour
oil for frying

1. In a bowl, mix the meat, egg, garlic and the bread which has been previously soaked in a little of the milk. Pour in the remainder of the milk, add the parsley, season and stir in the nutmeg and lemon peel.
2. Form the meat into small cakes 5 cm (2 in) in diameter.
3. Dust them with flour and fry them in the oil.
4. Serve with a tomato or potato salad.

The following are some of the variations. Use the same proportions as above.

Polpette de la serva: use a mixture of minced veal and pork with parsley and garlic.
Polpette di maiale: use pork and pork liver with breadcrumbs, grated cheese, parsley, sage, garlic, tomato and egg.
Polpette della nonna: use pickled pork and ham.
Polpette Campari: use minced pork and/or veal, bacon, bread, grated cheese, egg, onion, garlic, parsley, spices.

Costolette di maiale
Pork Chops, with Garlic and White Wine

Serves 4

4 or 8 pork chops, depending on size
1 tablespoon each of chopped fresh rosemary and sage
2 cloves garlic, crushed
salt

freshly ground black pepper
1 cup (8 fl oz) water
3 tablespoons butter
½ cup (4 fl oz) dry white wine

1. Rub the pork chops with a mixture of the herbs, garlic, salt and pepper and let them stand for 1 hour.
2. In a large frying pan, simmer the chops in the water and butter for 10 to 15 minutes until the water has evaporated, then let them brown in the butter.
3. Pour in the wine and simmer for a few minutes until the cooking juice thickens a little. Serve immediately.

Lesso misto con salsa verde

Mixed Boiled Meats with Green Sauce

This dish is known as bollito misto in other parts of Italy and is related to the French pot-au-feu. It can be an extravagant dish and is best suited for a large number of people since it requires quite a variety of different types of meat.

Serves 12

1 kg (2 lb) shin beef
4 veal shanks
4 pig's trotters
2 pig shanks
500 g (1 lb) cotecchino sausage, or
  similar
½ a calf's head
1 medium-size chicken
water
2 onions, studded with cloves
2 carrots, chopped
3 stalks celery, chopped
salt
12 whole black peppercorns

SALSA VERDE (GREEN SAUCE):
½ cup chopped parsley
2 pickled cucumbers, chopped
4 anchovy fillets, chopped
1 clove garlic, crushed
¼ cup (2 fl oz) olive oil
1-2 tablespoons red wine vinegar

1. The total cooking time of the dish is 2 to 2½ hours and the various meats should be added to the pot at different times as their cooking times vary.
   Start with the calf's head and beef. Half an hour later add the veal shanks, pig shanks and trotters, and allow approximately 1 hour for the chicken and sausage.
2. Place the meat in a large pot and add all the non-meat ingredients. Bring to the boil and simmer for 2 to 2½ hours. If necessary during the course of cooking, add more water.
3. Serve with boiled potatoes, or boiled white haricot beans. It is sometimes also served with stewed cabbage.
4. To make the green sauce, combine all the ingredients and serve separately.

Fegato di vitello alla milanese

Milanese Calves' Liver

Serves 4

750 g (1½ lb) calves' liver
½ cup chopped parsley
salt
freshly ground black pepper
¼ cup (2 fl oz) olive oil

½ cup (2 oz) flour
2 eggs, lightly beaten
½ cup (2 oz) fine dry breadcrumbs
125 g (4 oz) butter
4 lemon wedges

1. Cut the liver into slices 1.5 cm (½ in) thick and arrange them in a shallow dish.
2. Sprinkle with half the parsley, season and pour the oil over the top.
3. Marinate the liver for 1 hour.
4. Drain the liver, dust it with flour, dip it in the egg and then the breadcrumbs.
5. Fry the liver in the butter until it is golden-brown.
6. Just before it is cooked, add the remaining parsley to the butter.
7. To serve, pour the parsley butter over the liver.

Crott di Cameli, Dongo, Lake Como

*If it had not been for Guiseppe, the guide
from the tourist office, I would not have
discovered Crott di Cameli. Situated in an
ancient partly-abandoned hamlet in the hills
above Dongo, it is like a robbers' hideout. A
precarious walk through the empty alleys
which wind between deserted houses, gaping
with windowless openings, leads to the large
covered outdoor 'eating place' – to call it a
restaurant would be misleading. Next to it,
hugging the hillside, is an old stone building
and here, on several levels, the cooking is
done. If offered an inspection, decline; it may
put you off your food. However, what
emerges from these primitive cooking areas is
delicious if very basic food: spit-roasted lamb,
one or two pasta dishes with superb sauces,
trays of local sausages and prosciutto. I tried
their tripe soup and it was the most delicious
I have ever eaten. The wine was served in a
rough earthenware jug and it was as basic as
its container.*

Above: *A selection of local fish dishes
displayed on the terrace of Crotto del Misto
at Lezzeno against the background of
Lake Como.*

Right: *Host at Crott di Cameli taps wine
directly from the barrel into an
earthenware jug.*

Pizzette al Gorgonzola

Gorgonzola Biscuits

Makes 18 biscuits

90 g (3 oz) butter
185 g (6 oz) Gorgonzola cheese
2 cups (8 oz) flour
2 egg yolks, lightly beaten

¼ teaspoon nutmeg
salt
freshly ground black pepper
1 egg white, lightly beaten

1. Preheat oven to 230°C (450°F/Gas 8).
2. In a mixing bowl cream the butter and cheese, add the flour, egg yolks, nutmeg, salt and pepper.
3. Cover the dough with some plastic film and refrigerate for approximately 30 minutes.
4. Roll out the dough to a thickness of 6 mm (approx. ¼ in) and with a 7 cm (approx. 3 in) diameter biscuit cutter, cut it into circles.
5. Arrange the circles on a buttered and floured baking sheet.
6. Brush each biscuit with the egg white and bake in the preheated oven for approximately 15 to 20 minutes or until golden brown.
7. The biscuits are served cold with pre-dinner drinks.

Semifreddo di cioccolata

Chilled Chocolate Cream with Lady Fingers

Serves 4

125 g (4 oz) butter
½ cup (4 oz) sugar
2 egg yolks
¼ cup (1 oz) cocoa (if sweetened
  drinking chocolate powder is used,
  reduce the amount of sugar)

1-2 tablespoons milk
12 lady fingers, more if necessary
2 tablespoons chopped pistachio nuts
¼ cup (1 oz) hazelnuts, chopped and
  roasted

1. In a mixing bowl, cream the butter, add the sugar, egg yolks and the cocoa. Continue mixing for a few minutes and finally add some milk until the mixture is the consistency of thick cream.
2. In a decorative glass bowl, place a layer of lady fingers, spread them with some of the mixture and sprinkle with some of the pistachio nuts. Continue the layers finishing with a layer of the chocolate cream. Sprinkle the top with the hazelnuts and place the bowl in the freezer for 2 to 3 hours.

Budino di cioccolata

Chocolate Pudding

Serves 4

3 egg yolks
½ cup (4 oz) caster (powdered) sugar
250 g (8 oz) bitter (dark) chocolate,
  grated

185 g (6 oz) butter
1 cup (8 fl oz) cream, whipped
2 tablespoons hazelnuts, chopped

1. Cream the eggs with 5 tablespoons of the sugar until the mixture is smooth and almost white.
2. Melt the chocolate in a saucepan over a low heat, and then let it cool.
3. Cream the butter with the remaining sugar, beat in the egg mixture and the melted chocolate, and fold in the whipped cream.
4. Pour the mixture into an oiled pudding mould and refrigerate for 3 to 4 hours.
5. To serve, dip the mould in some warm water and unmould onto a serving platter. Garnish with the chopped hazelnuts.

Crema al mascarpone

Cream Cheese Dessert with Rum

Serves 4-6

500 g (1 lb) Mascarpone cheese or
  ricotta-type cream cheese
125 g (4 oz) caster (powdered) sugar
4 egg yolks

½ cup (4 fl oz) rum
juice ½ lemon
½ teaspoon cinnamon

1. In a bowl, cream the cheese, add the sugar, egg yolks, rum and lemon juice. This may be very sucessfully done in a food processor. Put all the ingredients together and blend until they are smooth and creamy.
2. To serve, place the cheese mixture in glass bowls. Refrigerate and then, just before serving, sprinkle with cinnamon.

Liguria

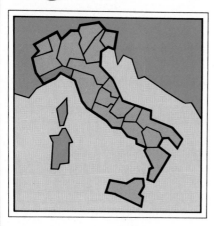

Liguria is a narrow strip of land on Italy's north-west coast. It is mountainous country and agriculture plays a very small part in the region's economy. Its most famous agricultural product is probably basil. This deliciously pungent herb grows all over the region and is the basis of the Ligurian sauce, pesto. Pesto is served on trenette, a type of ribbon pasta, floating on top of a bowl of minestrone (which Ligurians claim to have invented) or on potato gnocchi. It is a strongly flavoured sauce, too strong for some, but it can be toned down by adding cream.

Ravioli is said to have been invented in Liguria (or more correctly by Ligurian sailors at sea) as a way of making left-overs more palatable.

Naturally being a coastal province, much of Liguria's food comes from the sea. Fish soups and stews are popular and so, surprisingly for a region with such direct access to fresh fish, is dried and salted cod.

The most famous dish of Liguria is cappon magro, a pyramid of boiled vegetables and seafood. It is extremely elaborate, expensive and laborious to prepare, not the sort of thing you would make at home, but a dish that shouldn't be missed if you go to Genoa.

Cima alla genovese is another well-known dish of the region. It is shoulder or breast of veal, boned and stuffed with vegetables, herbs, pistachio nuts, hard-boiled eggs and chopped meat. It is served cold, cut into slices.

The story goes that Liguria's cuisine was shaped by its sailors. They were at sea for so long and their food was so monotonous that they craved fresh vegetables and herbs; they didn't want fish, they'd had enough of that, and they definitely didn't want any food that was spiced – many of the ships carried spices and the sailors breathed in their strong aroma for months on end.

This accounts for the Ligurian love of vegetables. They're quite often stuffed and baked and at Easter time they're made into a pie with hard-boiled eggs and a creamy sauce – torta pasqualina.

Tourism is one of Liguria's main industries. The drive along the coast is a breathtaking experience. The road takes you through many small towns and fishing villages, past fields of flowers and you can stop at any number of restaurants and cafés along the way, many of which specialise in regional food.

The quayside in Santa Marguerita, a well-known holiday resort on the Mediterranean.

Pesto
Ligurian Basil Sauce

From the pesto of the Ligurian coast is derived the pistou of the French Riviera. This recipe comes from Palma in Alassio. If you find the taste too pungent, add a little cream.

Makes 1½ cups (12 fl oz)

½ cup finely chopped fresh basil
3 cloves garlic
coarse salt
½ cup (2 oz) grated (Sardinian)
  pecorino cheese

½ cup (2 oz) grated Parmesan cheese
1 cup (8 fl oz) olive oil

1. Place all the ingredients except the oil in a mortar and grind to a paste.
2. Add the oil, drop by drop, until it becomes thick and smooth.
Note: Pesto is used as a sauce on any type of pasta or as a topping on soups, especially minestrone. In this case, it must not be cooked but placed on top of the soup when serving it in the soup plate.

Salsa genovese
Veal and Mushroom Sauce

Serves 4-6

1 onion, sliced
2-3 tablespoons butter
1 carrot, chopped
1 stalk celery, chopped
2 tablespoons dried mushrooms,
  previously soaked in water for 20
  minutes
250 g (8 oz) shoulder of veal, diced

3 tomatoes, peeled and chopped
1 tablespoon flour
1-1½ cups (8-12 fl oz) beef or veal
  stock
1 cup (8 fl oz) dry white wine
salt
freshly ground black pepper

1. Brown the onion in the butter, add the other vegetables except the tomatoes, then add the veal.
2. When the meat has browned, add the tomatoes, then the flour. Stir until the flour has amalgamated.
3. Slowly add the stock and the wine, season and cook for 30 minutes.
4. The sauce may either be strained or served with all its ingredients, and is especially good when served with any type of pasta.

Minestrone alla genovese

Genoese Vegetable Soup

Serves 4

¼ small cabbage, chopped
2 potatoes, diced
2 zucchinis (courgettes), sliced
½ cup fresh peas
2 small eggplants, (aubergines), diced
250 g (8 oz) green beans, cut into
   1.5 cm (½ in) pieces

1¼ cups (8 oz) dried beans, previously
   soaked for 12 hours
1 stalk celery, chopped
8-10 cups (2-2½ litres) water
salt
freshly ground black pepper

Combine all ingredients, add the water, season and simmer for 1 hour. Serve it with a spoonful of pesto (see p.120) on top. Do not cook the pesto.

Ravioli di magro

Ravioli Stuffed with Fish and Ricotta Cheese

Serves 6

STUFFING:
500 g (1 lb) white, firm non-fatty fish,
   grilled
1 bunch borage
1 small bunch fresh herbs such as
   oregano or marjoram, finely
   chopped
100 g (3½ oz) ricotta cheese
1 cup (4 oz) grated Parmesan cheese
2 whole eggs
¼ teaspoon salt
freshly ground black pepper

PASTA:
600 g (1 lb 3½ oz) flour
¾ cup (6 fl oz) water
½ cup (2 oz) grated Parmesan cheese

1. Remove all bones from the fish and mince it very finely.
2. Wash the borage and the herbs, remove the leaves and cook them in a little water for 3 to 4 minutes. Drain thoroughly, squeeze out all excess water and mince them very finely.
3. In a bowl, combine the minced fish and borage and herbs. Add the rest of the stuffing ingredients and mix together thoroughly until the texture is that of a very fine paste. A food processor is ideal for preparing this stuffing.
4. To make the pasta, place the flour on a wooden board and form a well. Add the salt to the lukewarm water and carefully combine with the flour to make a flexible dough.
5. Work the pasta vigorously for approximately 15 minutes.
6. Divide the pasta into 2 or 3 parts and roll one of them into a thin sheet. With a pastry wheel cut the sheet into 7 cm (3 in) wide strips.
7. With a teaspoon, place the stuffing approximately one finger's width apart on the lower half of the strip. Fold the upper half of the strip over the lower and firmly press it down so that it fuses with the lower. With the pastry wheel cut the strip into individual ravioli. Repeat the above with the remaining pasta.
8. In a large saucepan boil a generous amount of salted water and add the ravioli, a few at a time. Boil for approximately 15 minutes.
9. Serve sprinkled with grated Parmesan cheese.

Riso alla genovese
Rice with Veal Sauce

Serves 4

2 tablespoons butter
2 tablespoons olive oil
4 carrots, chopped
½ bunch celery, chopped
2 onions, chopped
500 g (1 lb) minced veal
salt

freshly ground black pepper
¾ cup (6 fl oz) dry white wine
3 tablespoons chopped fresh herbs
  (whichever type available)
1½-2 cups (9-12 oz) rice
½ cup (2 oz) grated Parmesan cheese

1. In the butter and oil sauté the carrots, celery and onions, add the meat and fry until it is brown, season and then add the wine and herbs.
2. Cover and simmer for 1 hour. If at the end it is too liquid, uncover and cook for a few minutes more.
3. In the meantime cook the rice in water. Be careful not to overcook. Drain, add some of the sauce and cook slowly for 5 minutes.
4. When serving, pour the rest of the sauce over each serving of rice and sprinkle with grated cheese.

Spinaci alla Liguria
Spinach with Pine Nuts and Raisins

Serves 4

1 kg (2 lb) spinach
2 tablespoons olive oil
1 clove garlic, crushed
4 slices bacon or 4 slices prosciutto
  crudo, chopped

2 tablespoons pine nuts
2 tablespoons raisins
2 tablespoons butter
salt
freshly ground black pepper

1. In a large saucepan, boil some salted water and cook the spinach in it for 5 minutes. Drain and rinse it under cold running water.
2. Roughly chop the spinach and sauté it in olive oil with the garlic and the bacon or prosciutto.
3. When cooked, add the pine nuts and raisins, stir in the butter and season it to taste.

Stufato di manzo alla genovese
Genoese Beef Stew

Serves 4

500 g (1 lb) onions, sliced
60 g (2 oz) butter
1 kg (2 lb) shin of beef or topside, in
  one piece
2 tomatoes, peeled and chopped
2 carrots, sliced

2 stalks celery, chopped
salt
freshly ground black pepper
1 cup (8 fl oz) dry white wine
1 tablespoon dried basil
2 cups (16 fl oz) water

1. In a heavy-bottomed casserole, fry the onions lightly in the butter. Add the meat and brown it on all sides then add the remaining ingredients.
2. Cook gently, covered for 2 to 3 hours. Serve from the casserole.

Palma, Alassio

Alassio is one of a group of Ligurian coastal towns which thrive during the tourist season and lead a dreamy existence enjoying the uncrowded winter sun of the Mediterranean. Nevertheless, with the exception of Genoa, few of them enjoy a reputation as great gourmet centres; and while they all serve good food, not many present local dishes. Among the few exceptions is Palma at Alassio. There, Fiorita and Silvio Viglietti offer delicious Ligurian dishes. Trenette con pesto, one of the most typical combinations of Ligurian regional cooking, is a tagliatelle-like ribbon pasta served with that unmistakably Ligurian sauce made of basil, coarse salt, garlic, pecorino, Parmesan, olive oil and sometimes pine nuts. I also tasted zimino, a seafood soup containing mussels, clams, octopus and calamari, cooked in oil with garlic, parsley and a combination of carrots, celery, tomato, onions, anchovies, basil and water. It is served with bruschetta, toasted bread with garlic and oil. Corsetti, which are figure eight-shaped pieces of pasta served with mushrooms and a sauce of garlic, rosemary, tomato and some dry white wine, were also delicious.

Above: *Clockwise from bottom left: botargo of tuna, trenette with pesto (see p.120); zimino (seafood soup); corsetti with mushrooms; tournados alla Palma.*

123

Vitello alla genovese
Veal Escalopes, Genoese Style

Serves 4

4 escalopes of veal, pounded thin
3 raw artichokes (if not available use
   tinned hearts)
1 tablespoon butter

1 cup (8 fl oz) dry white wine
salt
freshly ground black pepper

1. Prepare the veal as in the basic recipe of scaloppine alla milanese (see p. 108).
2. If using fresh artichokes, remove all the leaves, the choke and the stalk. Slice the heart into very thin slices and briefly and gently cook the slices in the butter.
3. Add the veal and brown them together for a few minutes. Add the wine and cook for 2 to 3 minutes.
4. Season and serve.

Cima alla genovese
Stuffed Shoulder or Breast of Veal

Serves 6-8

1.5-2 kg (3-4 lb) shoulder or breast of
   veal, boned
2 tablespoons butter
¼ cup (2 fl oz) olive oil
1 clove garlic, crushed
250 g (8 oz) veal, finely minced
155 g (5 oz) calves' or lambs' brains,
   chopped
155 g (5 oz) calves' or lambs'
   sweetbreads, chopped
salt
freshly ground black pepper
2 tablespoons fresh marjoram,
   chopped
½ cup (2 oz) fresh peas

60 g (2 oz) artichoke hearts, chopped
   (optional)
¼ cup (1 oz) grated Parmesan cheese
60 g (2 oz) shelled pistachio nuts
3 eggs, hard-boiled
8-12 cups (2-3 litres) veal stock; if not
   available, use water and add the
   following:
   1 large onion, chopped
   2 carrots, chopped
   1 stalk celery, chopped
   2 bay leaves
   12 peppercorns
   1 teaspoon salt

1. Ask the butcher to bone the shoulder or breast, making sure that it forms the largest possible flat piece.
2. Heat the butter and the oil. Add the garlic and sauté the minced veal, brains and sweetbreads. Season and add the marjoram. Cook until lightly browned.
3. If a food processor or mincer is available, process the meat mixture to fine texture.
4. In a bowl, mix the meat, peas, artichoke hearts, cheese and pistachio nuts. Taste, and if necessary, adjust the seasoning.
5. Spread the stuffing on the shoulder or breast, place the hard-boiled eggs in a row and roll the meat around the stuffing. Using twine, bind the roll and wrap it in cheesecloth.
6. Place the roll in a saucepan and cover it with veal stock.
7. Bring it to the boil, reduce the heat and simmer for 2 to 2½ hours. Cool the roll in the stock, remove it from the cooking liquid and refrigerate.
8. Carve the roll into slices to serve. It can also be eaten hot.

Arista alla genovese

Loin of Pork with Garlic and Rosemary

Serves 6

2 kg (4 lb) loin of pork
3 cloves garlic, cut into slivers
3-4 sprigs rosemary

4 tablespoons olive oil
salt
freshly ground black pepper

1. Preheat the oven to 180°C (350°F/Gas 4).
2. With a sharp knife cut small pockets in the meat and into each, insert a sliver of garlic and some rosemary.
3. Heat the oil in a heavy-bottomed roasting dish and brown the loin all over.
4. Season and place into the preheated oven.
5. Roast for approximately 1¼ hours, turning the loin from time to time to ensure that it browns evenly.
6. When cooked, let it stand for 5 minutes before carving it into slices. Serve it with the cooking juices poured over.

Pasta genovese

Genoese Sponge Cake

Makes one 20 cm (8 in.) cake.

4 eggs
125 g (4 oz) caster (powdered) sugar

1 cup (4 oz) flour
50 g (1½ oz) melted warm butter

1. Preheat oven to 180°C (350°F/Gas 4).
2. In a bowl, preferably copper, using a balloon whisk, beat the eggs and sugar over moderate heat, until double in volume.
3. Gradually, in small quantities add the flour and butter.
4. Pour the mixture into a round buttered springform pan.
5. Bake in the preheated oven for about 25-35 minutes.

Note: This is a basic sponge cake which may be cut horizontally and filled with various creams and decorated to your liking.

Piedmont and the Valle d'Aosta

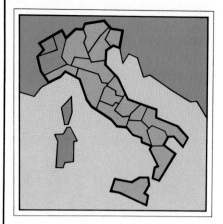

Piedmont's mountainous terrain produces many more crops than one would think possible. Turnips, potatoes, celery, cardoons and of course the famous white truffles all grow successfully here. So does barley and rye, and wine grapes are grown even at 1,000 metres.

Cardoons, which are from the same family as artichokes, grow to enormous size in Piedmont and are usually sliced and eaten raw, especially with bagna cauda, that deliciously pungent garlic and anchovy sauce.

Another Piedmont speciality is fonduta, a close relation to the Swiss fondue, made from fontina cheese. It is different from fondue in that it contains no alcohol and instead of being served from a common pot, it is poured into individual plates and topped with a layer of paper-thin slices of white truffle.

Polenta is also eaten frequently, especially with game. In the southern part of the province is the Po valley where rice is grown. And while there are many rice dishes in the Piedmont cuisine, pasta is still very popular, agnolotti in particular. As you would expect on a mountainous region, the swift streams produce excellent trout which are usually served very simply either fried or grilled.

Piedmont's capital city, Turin, unlike the capitals of most other regions, does not exercise a very strong gastronomic influence on the region as a whole. In fact it has been called 'the most Italian city of France' because its cuisine is so reminiscent of that of France. Nevertheless the city has some of the best restaurants of the region.

Piedmont is famous for its sweet dishes, unusual in Italy where most people finish off a meal with fruit or cheese. Puddings made from chocolate, chestnuts and hazelnuts are special favourites and the chocolates of Piedmont are well-known throughout Italy.

Most Piedmont wines are red; Barolo is the most famous and it's probably the best wine in the whole of Italy. But Piedmont is also the producer of the sparkling white wine, Asti Spumante. Most of Italy's vermouth is produced here, Cinzano, Martini & Rossi, Gancia and others. The interesting thing about vermouth companies is that they started out as small family affairs and now they're huge, but still family affairs. The formula for the flavourings that go into vermouth (it's a mixture of wine, brandy, herbs, spices and vegetables) is kept strictly secret, only known to one or two members of the family. Even when it is made in other countries, the flavourings are mixed in Piedmont and sent to the branches in sealed containers.

The Valle d'Aosta is harsh mountain country where soup and black bread form the mainstay of the diet. Game is plentiful here too, and is usually made into very rich dishes and eaten with potatoes which grow even at high altitudes.

Baci or chocolate kisses, known and loved all over the world are made in the Valle d'Aosta. And while the wines of this region are not very distinguished, its Grappa is considered to be excellent.

The Valle d'Aosta.

Bagna calda (or cauda)
Piedmontese Hot Anchovy and Garlic Dip

This recipe is from the Hotel Reale in Asti.
It was here that I tried fritto misto alla piedmontese, made with local sausage, veal cutlets, veal liver, apples, macaroons, brains and polenta.
This was followed by a dish of local mushrooms marinated in oil, lemon juice and fresh herbs. Throughout the meal we drank delicious local wines.
My host, the president of the local tourist office, told me with great pride that Garibaldi, Cavour and Tito Schipa had stayed at the Reale. I could see why.

Serves 6

VEGETABLES:
1 cauliflower, broken into bite-size flowerets
12 small button mushrooms
2 carrots, peeled and cut into thin strips about 5 cm (2 in) long
1 cucumber, peeled, seeded and cut into thin strips about 5 cm (2 in) long
1 red and 1 green pepper (capsicum), seeded and cut into thin strips

4 sticks celery, cut into thin strips about 5 cm (2 in) long
12 spring onions (scallions), trimmed to 5 cm (2 in) long
12 cherry tomatoes
12 radishes
SAUCE:
2 cups (16 fl oz) cream
60 g (2 oz) butter
12 anchovy fillets, finely chopped
1 clove garlic, crushed

1. Prepare the vegetables, place them in a bowl with water and refrigerate them for 2 hours.
2. In a saucepan, simmer the cream for 15 to 20 minutes until it has reduced to 1 cup.
3. In another saucepan, melt the butter, add the anchovies, garlic and then the reduced cream. Bring to simmering point but do not boil.
4. Arrange the vegetables on a serving platter with the sauce in an earthenware dish if available. To eat, dip the vegetables in the sauce.

Funghi ripieni alla piemontese
Piedmontese Stuffed Mushrooms

This recipe comes from La Maison de Filippo in Entrèves.

Serves 4 (as a first course)

4 very large or 8 medium-sized mushrooms
½ cup chopped parsley
4 anchovy fillets, finely chopped
2 onions, chopped

1 egg
½ cup (2 oz) fine dry breadcrumbs
2 tablespoons olive oil
salt
freshly ground black pepper

1. Preheat the oven to 180°C (350°F/Gas 4).
2. If possible, select large cup-shaped mushrooms, remove the stalks and chop them for the stuffing.
3. If you have a food processor, place all the ingredients except the whole mushrooms and the oil in the bowl and process to a fine texture. Otherwise mix the ingredients thoroughly in a bowl.
4. Fill the mushrooms with the mixture and sprinkle the tops with some of the oil.
5. Place the mushrooms on a baking tray and put them in the preheated oven for about 30 minutes. Check from time to time and if necessary sprinkle more oil on the mushrooms to prevent them drying out.

Cipolle ripiene alla piemontese
Piedmontese Stuffed Onions

Serves 4

4 medium-sized onions

STUFFING:
125 g (4 oz) macaroons
1 slice white bread, crusts removed
¼ cup (2 fl oz) milk
salt
freshly ground black pepper

⅛ teaspoon each of nutmeg, ground
**   cloves and cinnamon**
2 tablespoons grated Parmesan cheese
1 tablespoon sultanas
1 egg, lightly beaten
2 tablespoons butter

1. Preheat the oven to 190°C (375°F/Gas 5).
2. Boil the onions without peeling. When they have cooled, peel and cut them in half, and extract and reserve the core. Separate the individual layers.
4. To make the stuffing: Crumble the macaroons and pound them together with the bread which has been softened in the milk.
5. Season and add the spices, Parmesan, the chopped onion cores, sultanas and egg.
6. Place some of the stuffing into the hollow section of each onion and top with a knob of butter.
7. Place the onions on a baking tray and bake them in the preheated oven for 45 minutes. The onions may be eaten hot or cold.

Peperoni alla piemontese
Piedmontese Pimentos

Serves 4

4 pimentos
2 cloves garlic, crushed
4 tomatoes, peeled and chopped
4 fillets of anchovy, chopped

2 tablespoons butter, softened
4 tablespoons olive oil
salt
freshly ground black pepper

1. Preheat the oven to 180°C (350°F/Gas 4).
2. Cut the pimentos lengthwise in half, mix all the remaining ingredients and spoon the mixture into them.
3. Arrange the pimentos on a baking tray and bake them in the preheated oven for 30 minutes. They should not be overcooked.

Carciofi ripieni
Stuffed Artichokes

Serves 6

6 artichokes
salt
water
6 cloves garlic, peeled
6 tablespoons olive oil

STUFFING
1½ cups (6 oz) fine dry breadcrumbs
1½ cups (5½ oz) grated Parmesan
    cheese
¾ cup finely chopped parsley
salt
freshly ground black pepper

1. Preheat the oven to 190°C (375°F/Gas 5).
2. Trim the artichokes by cutting off the tips of each leaf with scissors. Cut the stems.
3. Parboil the artichokes for 10 minutes in salted water. Drain.
4. If necessary, remove the centre choke from each artichoke.
5. To prepare the stuffing: Mix together the breadcrumbs, Parmesan, parsley, salt and pepper.
6. Push the leaves apart and in between the leaves insert the stuffing.
7. On top of each artichoke place 1 clove of garlic.
8. Put the artichokes in a casserole dish, add water to a depth of approximately 2 cm (½ in) and pour 1 tablespoon of olive oil over each artichoke.
9. Cover the pot and place it in the preheated oven for 45 minutes or until the leaves easily pull away from the artichoke base. Before serving, remove the garlic clove.

Insalata alla moda d'Alba
Lettuce and Asparagus Salad

Serves 4

1 large fresh crisp lettuce
250 g (8 oz) fresh asparagus
2 stalks celery
250 g (8 oz) small button mushrooms
   (the original recipe calls for white
   truffles)

DRESSING:
½ cup (4 fl oz) olive oil
juice 1 lemon
salt
freshly ground black pepper
2 tablespoons cream

1. Remove the coarse outer leaves from the lettuce and carefully separate the remaining large leaves. Wash them and place them in the refrigerator for 1 to 2 hours so that they become crisp.
2. Trim the tough bottom ends of the asparagus and if necessary peel them. Bind them into a bundle and either steam them in an asparagus steamer or boil them, standing them vertically in a tall saucepan with about 5 cm (2 in) water in the bottom. Steam or boil for not more than 10 to 12 minutes. Cut off the tips about 7.5 cm (3 in) from the top for use in the salad and keep the rest for making an asparagus soup.
3. Cut the celery into 2 cm (¾ in) pieces, place them in a bowl of cold water and refrigerate them.
4. Finely slice the mushrooms.
5. Prepare the dressing in a screw top jar; combine all ingredients and shake thoroughly until it is emulsified.
6. On a decorative serving platter, arrange the whole lettuce leaves and on each, place some asparagus tips, chopped celery and sliced mushrooms. Pour some of the dressing over each salad.

La Maison de Filippo, Entrèves, Courmayeur

La Maison de Filippo looks very ancient and I was most surprised to hear that it was actually built in 1965 from the stones of a very old building which had stood there before. I was assured that it is a great sight to see it against the background of Mount Blanc. Unfortunately on the day of my visit, it poured with rain and the visibility was down to a few hundred metres. The restaurant, situated at the entrance to the Mount Blanc tunnel is very popular and caters for an impressive international clientele: President Giscard D'Estaing, the Queen of Denmark and other famous people come here to enjoy the food of the region. The interior looks like a very old farmhouse and most of the food presented is wholesome peasant fare. Most of the dishes on the menu are à la valdôtaine and La Maison de Filippo is among the few places in the world where you can eat chamois.

Above: *from bottom left: polenta; peperoni with garlic dip; potatoes; carbonata (spicy beef stew). Second step: prosciutto; boiled ham.*

Gnocchi alla piemontese

Potato Gnocchi

Serves 4

500 g (1 lb) potatoes, boiled and
    mashed
1-1½ cups (4-6 oz) flour
¾ cup (3 oz) grated Parmesan cheese

1 egg, lightly whisked
salt
pepper
¼ teaspoon nutmeg

1. Mix all the ingredients together in a large bowl. It should have a firm consistency. If it is too liquid, add more flour.
2. Refrigerate the mixture for 2 to 3 hours (this will make it easier to handle).
3. Make small balls of the mixture and roll them into cylinders in flour on a board.
4. Drop into a large pan of simmering salted water and cook gently for a few minutes until they rise to the surface.
5. Remove with a slotted spoon to a heated serving dish and serve with browned butter and freshly grated Parmesan.

Fonduta alla piemontese

Piedmontese Cheese Fondue

From the restaurant Teste Vin in Turin.
The owner of this restaurant, Piero Sattanino, has a very original way of serving his food and wine. He selects a different wine for each course and the diner is given a glass or two. This meant that during my excellent meal there, I had the opportunity to taste a variety of wines which I normally could not attempt in a single meal.

Serves 4

410 g (13 oz) fontina cheese, diced
1 cup (8 fl oz) milk
30 g (1 oz) butter

4 egg yolks
1 truffle from Alba (optional)
thin slices of toast

1. Place the cheese in a bowl and cover it with milk. Leave to stand for 2 to 3 hours.
2. In a fire-proof dish, melt the butter, and over a moderate heat add the cheese and milk, stirring continuously with a whisk until the cheese has completely melted.
3. Increase the heat and continue to stir while adding the egg yolks one after another, mix well. Turn down the heat and cook until the mixture is creamy.
4. Pour the fondue into four individual dishes and cover them with very finely sliced truffles. Serve with thin slices of toast.

Note: If truffles are not available, thin slices of champignon-type mushrooms may be served.

Pollo alla Marengo

Chicken Marengo

Serves 4

1 chicken, about 1.5 kg (3 lb)
2 tablespoons butter
½ cup (4 fl oz) olive oil
salt
freshly ground black pepper
1 clove garlic, chopped
1 onion, sliced
1 stalk celery, chopped
250 g (8 oz) button mushrooms, sliced
4 tomatoes, peeled and chopped

¼ teaspoon thyme
1 bay leaf
1½ cups (12 fl oz) dry white wine
½ cup (4 fl oz) brandy
½ cup chopped parsley
4 large raw prawns, peeled and
  de-veined
4 slices white bread, crusts removed
4 eggs

1. Cut the chicken into pieces.
2. Heat the butter and half the oil in a large saucepan and brown the pieces of chicken. Season well.
3. Add the garlic, onion and celery and sauté for a few minutes, then add the mushrooms, tomatoes, thyme and bay leaf. Pour in the wine and brandy, and add half the parsley. Simmer for 20 minutes.
4. Add the prawns and cook for 2 to 3 minutes, remove and set aside.
5. In the remaining oil, fry the slices of bread and, separately, the eggs.
6. To serve, place the chicken pieces in the centre of a large serving platter and around them arrange alternately the fried bread with the eggs and prawns on top. Spoon the cooking juices over the chicken.

Costoletti di vitello con fontina (alla valdostana)

Veal Chops with Fontina Cheese from the Aosta Valley

This recipe is from Cavallo Bianco in Aosta (also known as Cheval Blanc in this French-speaking region). It is a picturesque old holstelry built on top of Roman vaulted cellars which today store some very fine regional wines.
The restaurant specialises in regional dishes. Fontina cheese is used extensively and soups and stews feature regularly on the menu.

Serves 4

4 veal chops, about 2 cm (¾ in) thick
4 slices fontina cheese (Gruyère-type
  cheese may be used instead)
salt
freshly ground black pepper
¼ cup (1 oz) flour

2 eggs, lightly beaten
1 cup (4 oz) fine dry breadcrumbs
125 g (4 oz) butter
1 tablespoon finely chopped rosemary
2 tablespoons brandy

1. In each veal chop cut a horizontal pocket and insert a slice of cheese. Season with salt and pepper.
2. Dust the chops with flour, dip them in the eggs and then the breadcrumbs.
3. Melt the butter in a frying pan and fry the chops for approximately 10 minutes or until they are golden-brown.
4. Just before they are ready, sprinkle them with the rosemary and pour in the brandy. Season to taste and serve the chops with the sauce poured over them.

Venezia

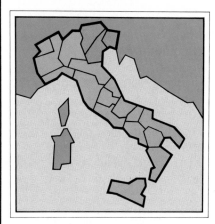

The region of Venezia is made up of three areas: Venezia Euganea or Veneto, of which Venice is the capital; Venezia Tridentina, to the west, whose customs and food have been greatly influenced by Austria, its neighbour; and Venezia Giulia, to the east of Veneto, a poor mountainous region adjacent to Yugoslavia and Austria. Of these, Veneto is the most gastronomically interesting and Venice is to a large part responsible for that.

Venice, once wealthy, powerful and magnificent, has faded somewhat and today it is like a valuable and well-loved antique, worn but cared for. Its architecture, twisting alleys and canals combine to give Venice its unique appearance. Adored throughout the ages, it has an atmosphere and feeling unknown in any other city. Its admirers are innumerable and today, as in the past, they flock to Venice. As a trader with the Orient during a period of almost one thousand years, Venice has been responsible for the introduction of many exotic foods, especially eastern spices and condiments. And, as you would expect from a coastal city, seafood plays a very important part in its cuisine. Scampi alla veneziana is one of its most widely known specialities. It is simply raw prawns, boiled, cooled and served with a vinaigrette made from olive oil, lemon juice, pepper and salt.

Seafood combines with rice in many Venetian dishes: risotto alla marinara (with clams), risi e bisati (with sole); risotto di mare (with lobster, prawns etc.) and risotto nero (black rice, made with the ink of the squid). The rice is grown along the banks of the Po river and forms the basis of many of Venice's most famous foods. Risi e bisi (rice and peas) sounds simple, even boring, but when prepared in Venice in the spring when peas are young and sweet and eaten on its own as a first course, it is a delicate and delicious dish.

After risi e bisi, Venice's most famous dish is probably fegato alla veneziana. This is tender, very thin slices of calves' liver, cooked briefly with onions which have been softened and lightly browned for about half an hour in a covered pan.

The cuisine of Venice is distinctive and dominant, but Verona, Vicenza, Padua and Treviso have developed their own specialities too and together they make the cuisine of Venezia one of the most interesting in Italy.

One of the many beautiful canals in Venice bathed in the golden evening light.

Zuppa di pollo

Chicken Soup

Serves 6

1 chicken, about 1.5 kg (3 lb)
3 bay leaves
2 tablespoons finely chopped herbs
  (fresh thyme, oregano or marjoram)
salt
freshly ground black pepper
2 tablespoons butter

3 carrots, chopped
½ bunch celery, chopped
3 potatoes, diced
2 leeks (white part only), thinly sliced
300 g (10 oz) fresh or frozen peas
6 slices toasted croûtons
½ cup (2 oz) grated Parmesan cheese

1. Put the chicken into a saucepan with enough water to cover. Add the bay leaves, herbs, salt and pepper.
2. Bring it slowly to the boil and simmer for 1 hour. Skim the surface.
3. In the butter sauté all the vegetables except the peas and add them to the saucepan with the chicken. Simmer for a further ½ hour then add the peas. (If raw, simmer for 10 minutes; if deep-frozen, cook for 3 minutes only.)
4. Remove the chicken, take the meat off the bone, keeping it in fairly large pieces.
5. Return the meat to the saucepan. Heat gently and serve with the toasted croûtons and grated cheese.

Risi e bisi

Venetian Rice and Peas

A famous dish of the Veneto region. It is a vegetable dish, not a soup, to be eaten with a fork, not a spoon.

Serves 4

1 onion, chopped
60 g (2 oz) ham, chopped
45 g (1½ oz) butter
375 g (12 oz) shelled peas
3 cups (24 fl oz) chicken stock or meat
  stock (water will produce a less rich
  dish)

2 cups (12 oz) rice
¼ cup (1 oz) grated Parmesan cheese

1. Sauté the onion and the ham in half the butter.
2. Add the peas, mix them well with the butter and add 1 cup of the stock or water.
3. When it starts to boil, add the rice and another cup of liquid. As it is absorbed keep adding more liquid. This will take approximately 12 to 15 minutes.
4. Limit the stirring to the minimum, so that the peas are not squashed. The final result should not be too liquid as the dish is meant to be eaten with a fork.
5. When the rice is cooked, stir in the rest of the butter and the cheese. Serve more of the Parmesan separately.

Risotto con le zuchete
Risotto with Zucchini

From Locanda Cipriani in Torcello, a one-star restaurant which has attracted the great and the famous for many years. Pleasant surroundings, discreet service and excellent regional food is what the Locanda Cipriani is all about.
Its fish dishes are particularly good and a raspberry dessert I had here – crostata di lamponi – was superb.

Serves 4

45 g (1½ oz) bacon, finely chopped
1 onion, chopped
½ clove garlic, chopped
315 g (10 oz) small zucchinis
  (courgettes), sliced
salt
freshly ground black pepper

1½ cups (9 oz) rice
approximately 4 cups (1 litre) chicken
  stock
¼ cup chopped parsley
3 tablespoons grated Parmesan cheese
30 g (1 oz) butter

1. Fry the bacon in a casserole, add the onion and garlic and sauté until light brown.
2. Add the zucchinis, salt and pepper and sauté until light brown.
3. Add the rice, stir, and add the chicken stock a little at a time. Keep adding the stock until the rice is completely cooked. Add the parsley.
4. When the rice is cooked add the grated cheese and butter.
5. Stir well and serve while hot.

Risotto nero
Black Risotto

A speciality of Harry's Bar in Venice.
Undoubtedly, Harry's Bar is among the most famous restaurants on Italy. Its fame started in the years immediately after the war when visiting Americans made it their home-away-from-home, complete with dry martinis. It is a modest, unassuming place run by Arrigo Cipriani. The food is exceptional.
On my visit here I ate the famous black risotto and filetto carpacio, paper-thin slices of raw yearling beef served with a mayonnaise-type sauce. I drank Prosecco, a sparkling dry wine served, with the ultimate touch of elegance, in a Venetian glass jug.

Serves 4

1 kg (2 lb) cuttlefish
8 tablespoons olive oil
½ onion, finely chopped
1 clove garlic, peeled
¼ cup chopped parsley
½ cup (4 fl oz) dry white wine

1½ cups (9 oz) rice
2 tablespoons tomato purée
3-4 cups (24-32 fl oz) fish stock
salt
pepper

1. Remove the ink bag from the cuttlefish and reserve it.
2. Cut the cuttlefish into short lengths.
3. In a casserole, sauté the onion and garlic in the oil. Remove the garlic when it is brown. Add the parsley and cuttlefish and sauté it for 10 to 15 minutes.
4. Pour in the wine and add the ink. Sauté for a further 5 minutes.
5. Stir in the rice, add the tomato purée, and add the boiling fish stock, a spoonful at a time, until the rice is completely cooked.
6. Season to taste before serving.

Risotto di mare

Seafood Risotto

Serves 4

2 blue swimmer crabs or 1 small
   crayfish, cooked
500 g (1 lb) shelled school prawns
   (shrimps), cooked
2 carrots, chopped
2 stalks celery, chopped
1 onion, chopped
2 tablespoons butter

3 tablespoons olive oil
3 tablespoons chopped parsley
2 cups (12 oz) rice
salt
freshly ground black pepper
½ cup (4 fl oz) dry white wine
approximately 2 cups (16 fl oz) fish
   stock

1. Chop the crab and prawns.
2. Sauté the carrots, celery and onion in the butter and oil, add the parsley and the rice and season.
3. Gradually add sufficient wine and fish stock to cook the rice. Simmer until the rice is cooked and the liquid has been absorbed.
4. Stir in the seafood and cook for another 5 minutes. Season.

Risotto di pesce a la ciosota

Risotto with Fish Stock and Wine

This is one of the most famous and delicious of Venetian rice dishes and there are many ways of preparing it – some maintain that cheese should be added at the end.
It is a speciality of Al Nonno Risorto in Venice, a modest trattoria where authentic regional food is served. Here I have eaten eel stewed in a tomato-based sauce (anguilla in umido); thin strips of liver cooked with onions and served with polenta (fegato alla veneziana) and this recipe, which like the others, is delicious.

Serves 4

¼ cup (2 fl oz) olive oil
1 clove garlic
1 onion, sliced
½ cup chopped parsley
500 g (1 lb) go fish (gudgeon from
   Venetian Lagoon) or any type of
   white-fleshed fish can be used

salt
4 cups (1 litre) water
60 g (2 oz) butter
1½ cups (9 oz) rice
½ cup (4 fl oz) dry red wine
freshly ground black pepper

1. In a heavy-bottomed casserole, in the olive oil, fry the garlic together with the onion and half the parsley.
2. Add the fish and salt to taste, cover with water and boil for 20 minutes.
3. Strain through a sieve while pressing with a wooden spoon to extract as much liquid as possible. Save the cooking liquid.
4. In a separate pan, melt half the butter, add the rice and stir.
5. With a ladle, add the fish stock, stir and continue adding the stock which will be absorbed as the rice cooks. If necessary, season with salt.
6. Add the wine and cook until it has evaporated.
7. Add the remaining butter and some freshly ground pepper together with the rest of the parsley. Stir and serve hot.

Dodici Apostoli, Verona

Under the professional guidance of Giorgio and Franco Gioco, the Dodici Apostoli has gained the reputation as one of the best restaurants in Italy. My first visit goes back to 1965, and the memory of my luncheon there was still quite fresh when I returned in 1979. Giorgio Gioco (above with a beautiful display of fruit) is in charge of the kitchen and is the author of a number of Italian cookbooks. He is also very proficient in the French répertoire, but his true love is for the local dishes of Verona and of Veneto. The restaurant is located in a little alley in the historical centre of the town just around the corner from the Piazza delle erbe, the ancient vergetable market. The Dodici Apostoli, with its painted walls, has the atmosphere of a Renaissance palazzo and the food is presented with a splendour worthy of that great period.

Risotto in capro roman

Venetian Risotto with Lamb

Serves 4

1 onion, chopped
2 tablespoons butter
2 tablespoons oil
250 g (8 oz) lean lamb (or mutton),
   diced
3 tomatoes, skinned and chopped

1 cup (8 fl oz) dry white wine
salt
freshly ground black pepper
beef stock
2 cups (12 oz) rice
¼ cup (1 oz) grated Parmesan cheese

1. Sauté the onion in the butter and oil, then add the meat and brown it.
2. Add the tomatoes, wine and season with salt and pepper. Pour in ½ cup of stock.
3. Cover the saucepan and simmer until the meat is cooked, approximately 20 minutes. Stir in the rice.
4. Let the rice absorb the cooking liquid then add more stock, and continue in this way until the rice is cooked. Make sure that the end result is not too wet. This will take 12 to 15 minutes.
5. Add the cheese just before serving.

Canederli tirolesi

Tirolean Dumplings

This recipe comes from the Hotel Grief in Bolzano.

Makes 36 dumplings

4 eggs
¾ cup (6 fl oz) milk
125 g (4 oz) butter
75 g (2½ oz) prosciutto, finely chopped
3 slices salami, finely chopped
1 onion, chopped

2 tablespoons parsley, chopped
6 cups stale bread, diced
3 tablespoons flour
salt
freshly ground black pepper
½ cup (2 oz) grated Parmesan cheese

1. In a mixing bowl, beat the eggs and the milk with a pinch of salt. Add the diced bread and soak for 20 minutes to absorb all the milk.
2. Sauté the prosciutto, salami, onion and parsley in half the butter, drain off any superflous fat and add the mixture to the bread.
3. Add the flour, stir gently and season.
4. In your hand, shape one tablespoon of the mixture at a time into a ball. Check that the mixture is of the right consistency by dropping the first dumpling gently into boiling water. If it breaks up, add more flour.
5. Place the dumplings, a few at a time, into the boiling water with a slotted spoon. Remove them as they rise to the surface.
6. To serve, melt the remaining butter, place the dumplings on individual plates, pour the butter over them and serve with grated Parmesan.

Polenta pastizzada
Polenta with Veal and Chicken Giblets

This recipe comes from Al Nonno Risorto in Venice.

Serves 6

185 g (6 oz) butter
410 g (13 oz) ripe tomatoes, peeled and
  mashed
1 onion, sliced
1 carrot, sliced
60 g (2 oz) celery stalks, chopped
220 g (7 oz) veal shoulder, cut into
  small cubes
½ cup (4 fl oz) dry white wine

30 g (1 oz) dried mushrooms, softened
  in hot water
salt
90 g (3 oz) chicken giblets, chopped
500 g (1 lb) polenta maize meal
7 cups (1.75 litres) water
90 g (3 oz) Gruyère cheese, cut into
  slices

1. Preheat the oven to 200°C (400°F/Gas 6).
2. Melt 60 g of the butter and fry the tomatoes, onion, carrot and celery.
3. Add the veal and brown it.
4. Add the wine and cook until it has reduced by approximately three-quarters, then add the mushrooms. Cover the casserole, lower the heat and simmer for 30 minutes.
5. In the remaining butter, brown the chicken giblets.
6. Prepare the polenta by cooking the polenta maize meal in the boiling water for about 1 hour, stirring often. When cooked, spread out the polenta on a board or tray to a thickness of approximately 1.5 cm (½ in). It will harden as it cools.
7. Grease an oven dish and place some of the polenta on the bottom of it.
8. Sprinkle the top of the polenta with some of the sauce prepared above, not using the chicken giblets. On top of the sauce place some slices of Gruyère. On top of that, arrange another layer of polenta, dot it with knobs of butter and distribute the browned chicken giblets on it. Cover it with more Gruyère. Continue the layers until all the ingredients are used and the dish is full. Dot the top layer with more knobs of butter.
9. Place the dish in the preheated oven for 15 to 25 minutes. It will be ready when the top has browned.
10. It is traditional to serve this dish with a good robust red wine.

Suppli al telefono
Rice and Cheese Balls

Suppli are so called because when broken open, the cheese inside the balls forms wire-like strands.

Serves 4-6

2 eggs
2 cups risotto (use left-overs, if
  available)
125 g (4 oz) mozzarella or Bel Paese
  cheese, cut into 1.5 cm (½ in) cubes

¾ cup (3 oz) dried breadcrumbs
olive or vegetable oil for frying

1. Lightly whisk the eggs and gently add them to the risotto.
2. Take 1 tablespoon of risotto and put it on the palm of your hand.
3. Place a cube of cheese on top of the rice, and place another tablespoon of rice on top of the cheese. Form into a ball.
4. Roll each ball carefully in the breadcrumbs.
5. Fry them in hot oil and drain well.
6. Serve as a first course for lunch or dinner.

Carciofi alla veneziana
Venetian Artichokes

From the Gritti Palace in Venice.

Serves 4

8-12 small artichokes
½ cup (4 fl oz) olive oil
½ cup (4 fl oz) dry white wine

½ cup (4 fl oz) water
salt
freshly ground black pepper

1. Trim off all the outer leaves of the artichokes so that only the tender inner leaves remain.
2. Put the artichokes into a large braising pan and cover them with the oil, wine and water. Season.
3. Cover the pan and stew them gently for 1 hour.
4. Remove the cover, turn up the heat and cook until the liquid is reduced and only the oil is left.
5. Serve with the oil poured over the artichokes.

Patate alla triestina
Trieste Potato Cake

From the Park Hotel Obelisco in Trieste.
The Obelisco serves regional food which means that it often seems more Austrian or Yugoslav than Italian. Their jota triestina, which is a bean, potato and cabbage soup, is very similar to a Yugoslavian dish, while their excellent tarts – especially those made from almonds – taste similar to those found in Austria.

Serves 4-6

1.75 kg (3½ lb) potatoes
salt
90 g (3 oz) bacon, finely chopped
30 g (1 oz) butter

2 tablespoons olive oil
1 onion, thinly sliced
½ cup (4 fl oz) beef stock

1. Boil the potatoes in salted water until they are tender.
2. Drain, peel and cut them into slices.
3. Lightly sauté the bacon in the butter and oil, add the onion and sauté until golden brown.
4. Add the potatoes, season and add the beef stock.
5. With the back of a fork, crush the potatoes roughly.
6. Over a low heat, cook the potatoes until the underside is brown.
7. Slide the potato cake onto a plate and reverse the sides. Fry again, adding more butter if necessary, until the second side is brown and crisp.

Gritti Palace, Venice

The Gritti Palace labels itself as the 'legendary palace of kings, writers and lovers' and one can justifiably add 'and gourmets'. It has the reputation of having some of the best food in Italy, preparing local specialities as well as national dishes. Every year the Gritti conducts a series of cooking seminars which attract lovers of Italian food from all over the world. The hotel is situated in a real palazzo which was built in the 15th century and belonged to the Doge Andrea Gritti.

Above: *the famous Gritti Palace summer buffet of antipasti.*
Right: *a selection of superb food from Harry's Bar. Clockwise from bottom left: green pasta, meringue cakes, black risotto (see p.137), raw beef.*

Papriche veneziane
Braised Peppers (Capsicums)

This recipe comes from Restaurante Marconi in Verona.
It's an elegant restaurant, situated behind Verona's most famous tourist attraction, Juliet's house.
Verona is well-known for its vegetables and the Marconi specialises in vegetable antipasto.
Vegetables are also used to make stuffings for pasta. And they're served very simply too: for
example, local mushrooms are fried in olive oil and served with fresh herbs and lemon juice.

Serves 6

½ cup (4 fl oz) olive oil
1 clove garlic, peeled
1 kg (2 lb) green and red peppers
  (capsicums), seeded and cut into
  strips

1 kg (2 lb) tomatoes, peeled and
  roughly chopped
salt
freshly ground black pepper
3 sprigs parsley, finely chopped

1. In a large pan, heat the olive oil and fry the clove of garlic until brown. Discard the garlic.
2. Add the peppers and gently simmer them for 15 minutes.
3. Add the tomatoes, salt and pepper and simmer until the mixture is reduced to a thick sauce.
4. Serve hot or cold sprinkled with parsley.

Frittata con piselli
Green Pea Omelette

Serves 4

75 g (2½ oz) butter
1 onion, finely chopped
60 g (2 oz) prosciutto, finely chopped
1 bulb fennel, finely sliced
250 g (8 oz) shelled green peas

salt
freshly ground black pepper
7 eggs, lightly beaten
3 sprigs parsley, finely chopped

1. Melt 60 g of the butter in a large frying pan, add the onion, prosciutto, fennel and peas and sauté lightly.
2. Season and add 1 cup of water.
3. Simmer for approximately 5 minutes, until the fennel is tender.
4. Drain the water, add the remaining butter, pour in the beaten eggs and add the parsley. Fry until it is brown.
5. Slip the omelette on to a large dinner plate, then turn it over and cook the other side until it is brown.
6. Cut the omelette into four and serve the quarters hot with a mixed green salad.

Ostriche alla veneziana
Oysters Venetian Style

Serves 4

¼ cup parsley, finely chopped
½ stalk celery, finely chopped
1 tablespoon finely chopped fresh
  oregano, thyme or marjoram

½ cup (2 oz) fine dry breadcrumbs
olive oil
juice 2 lemons
2 dozen oysters in their shells

1. Make a mixture of all the ingredients except the oil, lemon juice and oysters.
2. Put a little of it on each oyster in its shell.
3. Sprinkle with a few drops of oil and place them for a few minutes under a grill.
4. Sprinkle with lemon juice before serving.

Peòci al pangrattato
Mussels Venetian Style

Serves 4

1 cup finely chopped parsley
3 cloves garlic, finely chopped
1 cup (4 oz) fine dry breadcrumbs
salt

freshly ground black pepper
¼ cup (2 fl oz) olive oil
2 kg (4 lb) mussels, scrubbed

1. Combine the parsley, garlic, breadcrumbs, salt and pepper.
2. In a saucepan large enough to contain the mussels, heat most of the oil. Add the mussels, cover the pan, and heat until all the shells have opened. Remove one half-shell from each mussel and reserve the mussel liquid.
3. Place some of the breadcrumb mixture on top of each mussel in its shell, sprinkle with the remaining oil and place them under the grill to brown the breadcrumbs.
4. Serve with some of the mussel liquid poured over.

Baccalà alla vicentina
Vincenza Salt Cod

Serves 4

1 kg (2 lb) salt cod
¼ cup (2 fl oz) olive oil
2 tablespoons butter
2 onions, sliced
1 clove garlic, crushed

4 anchovy fillets, chopped
¼ teaspoon cinnamon
½ cup (4 fl oz) dry white wine
1-2 cups (8-16 fl oz) hot milk
½ cup (2 oz) grated Parmesan cheese

1. Soak the cod in cold water for several hours, changing the water often. This will remove its salty taste.
2. Drain the fish, skin and bone it.
3. Heat the oil and butter and add the onions, garlic and anchovies and sauté for a few minutes.
4. Cut the fish into pieces and put them into the saucepan. Add the cinnamon, wine and sufficient hot milk to cover.
5. Stew for 2 to 3 hours: by then the sauce should be reduced and thick. Before serving, mix in the cheese. Serve with toasted squares of polenta.

Baccalà mantecato
Cream of Salt Cod

From the Hotel Lido in Muggia, near Trieste.
Muggia is a picturesque fishing village and the Hotel Lido has a reputation for its seafood which the local fishermen supply fresh every day.
Scampi are simply boiled and served with oil, pepper and salt. Sea bass is boiled, grilled or roasted. Antipasto misto de mare, which includes any seafood that is available on the day, looks more elaborate, but the individual dishes are simple.

Serves 4

750 g (1½ lb) best quality salt cod
milk (if required)
4-6 tablespoons olive oil

1. Soak the cod in water until it has lost some of its toughness, changing the water often to remove its salty taste.
2. Steam it for 1 hour, then remove all bones and the skin.
3. Traditionally the cod is pounded in a mortar until it forms a thick creamy mass. The same result can be easily achieved in a food processor.
4. When pounding or processing it, add a few tablespoons of oil. If the fish is not sufficiently fat, it may require the addition of some warm milk to turn it to a soft purée.
5. Serve the cod with slices of polenta.

Hotel Grief, Bolzano

I first stayed at the Hotel Grief in 1962, and the things I remember most were the Steinpilze, large local mushrooms which were served grilled, cut into slices, and sprinkled with oil. The flavour was unforgettable. When I returned in 1979, it happened that on the day of my arrival, the hotel had just received a fresh delivery of this now so difficult to obtain delicacy. The chef obliged by serving them in this simple but delicious way. Regional cooking in Bolzano is of Austrian origin, and the antipasto dishes contain Speck, Bauern-Fleisch and gekochter Schinken, while pork dishes, game, and other main courses are served with Knödel and cabbage. Desserts are Apfelstrudel and Schmarren, the Austrian version of pancakes. It is not Italian cooking, but it's delicious.

Above: *clockwise from bottom left: Bolzano antipasto (selection of smoked meats); saddle of venison; forest berry dessert cup.*

Anguilla in umido

Eel Casserole

From Al Nonno Risorto in Venice.

Serves 4

3 tablespoons olive oil
2 cloves garlic, crushed
1 onion, sliced
800 g (1 lb 10 oz) eel, cleaned and cut
  into pieces

⅓ cup (2½ fl oz) white wine
1¼ cups (10 fl oz) fresh tomato purée
2 tablespoons chopped parsley
salt
freshly ground pepper

1. Heat the oil in a casserole dish, add the garlic and onion and brown them.
2. Add the eel and the wine and cook until the wine has almost evaporated. Add the tomato purée, parsley, salt and pepper.
3. Cover the casserole and continue cooking slowly for approximately 20 minutes, stirring occasionally. Serve as soon as it is cooked.

Pollo allo spiedo con riso in peverada

Spit-Roasted Chicken with Piquant Rice

Guinea fowl is sometimes used instead of chicken in this dish

Serves 4

1 chicken, about 1.5 kg (3 lb)
salt
freshly ground black pepper
2 tablespoons olive oil
2 cups (12 oz) rice

PEVERADA SAUCE:
125 g (4 oz) chicken livers, chopped
4 anchovy fillets, chopped
1 clove garlic, crushed
125 g (4 oz) pickled green peppers,
  chopped
¼ cup (2 fl oz) olive oil
salt
freshly ground black pepper
2 tablespoons chopped parsley
¼ cup (2 fl oz) chicken stock
juice 1 lemon
1 tablespoon white wine vinegar

1. Preheat the oven to 190°C (375°F/Gas 5).
2. Rub the chicken inside and out with salt and pepper and smear the outside with the oil. Place it in the preheated oven and spit-roast for 1¼ to 1½ hours. Baste frequently with the pan juices.
3. To make the sauce, place the chicken livers, anchovies, garlic and green peppers in a saucepan and sauté them in the oil, add the seasoning and the parsley.
4. Gradually add the stock, and simmer for 20 minutes. Add the lemon juice and vinegar.
5. Boil the rice in salted water until tender.
6. To serve, mix the peverada sauce into the rice. Serve the chicken carved into pieces surrounded by the rice.

Anatra in salsa piccante
Duck in Piquant Sauce

Serves 4

60 g (2 oz) butter
60 g (2 oz) bacon, finely chopped
1 sprig rosemary, finely chopped
3 sprigs sage, finely chopped
2 kg (4 lb) duck
1 lemon, cut into quarters
salt
freshly ground black pepper

1 tablespoon olive oil
185 g (6 oz) pork and veal mixture,
  finely minced
1 clove garlic, crushed
2 anchovy fillets, finely chopped
½ cup (4 fl oz) white wine vinegar
½-1 cup (4-8 fl oz) beef stock

1. Preheat oven to 220°C (425°F/Gas 7).
2. In a deep heavy casserole dish, melt the butter, add the bacon, rosemary and sage and fry for a few minutes.
3. Add the duckling and the lemon quarters and season with pepper and salt.
4. Place the casserole in the preheated oven and roast for approximately 30 minutes.
5. Take the casserole out of the oven and pour off the excess fat.
6. Return the casserole and roast it for a further 30 minutes, basting it with the cooking liquid.
7. In a heavy-bottomed frying pan, heat the oil and fry the minced meat, garlic and anchovy fillets until brown. Add the vinegar and the beef stock and cook until the liquid has reduced a little.
8. Remove the casserole from the oven, skim off the excess fat and cut the duckling into serving pieces.
9. Return them to the casserole and pour the minced meat sauce over it.
10. Reduce the heat to 150°C (300°F/Gas 2). Cover the casserole and return it to the oven to braise for 30 minutes.
11. Before serving, season and add more beef stock if necessary.

Fegato alla veneziana
Liver Venetian Style

This recipe comes from Al Nonno Risorto in Venice.

Serves 4

¼ cup (2 fl oz) olive oil
30 g (1 oz) butter
¼ cup chopped parsley
500 g (1 lb) onions, finely sliced
600 g (1 lb 3 oz) calves' liver, thinly
  sliced

4 tablespoons demi-glace or
  concentrated beef stock
salt
4 slices white bread, fried in butter
  and each cut in four

1. Place the oil and the butter in a large frying pan and when hot, add the parsley and then the onions. Stir, cover and very slowly cook for approximately half an hour.
2. Turn up the heat, add the liver, stir, add the demi-glace or beef stock and cook for no more than 5 minutes. It is important that the liver is just set and not cooked too much, otherwise it will be tough and dry.
3. Add the salt, stir, and transfer to a hot serving dish.
4. Traditionally the liver is served garnished with the fried bread and served with potato purée or hot polenta.

Crema fritta all veneta
Venetian Deep Fried Custard Pieces

Serves 4

2 cups (16 fl oz) milk
1 teaspoon vanilla essence
½ cup (4 oz) sugar
100 g (3½ oz) flour
salt
4 whole eggs

4 egg yolks
100 g (3½ oz) butter
fine breadcrumbs
oil for deep frying
icing (confectioners') sugar

1. Boil the milk and add the vanilla essence.
2. In a saucepan combine the sugar, flour, salt, 2 eggs and 4 egg yolks.
3. Beat in the hot milk, and heat it over a moderate flame stirring constantly until the mixture is very thick and smooth.
4. Remove from the heat and mix in 2 tablespoons of butter, making sure that it is well incorporated.
5. Pour the mixture in a shallow baking tray in a 1½ cm (approximately ½ in) layer. Melt the remaining butter and pour it over the custard cream.
6. Chill it and cut it into 4 cm (1½ in) squares or diamonds.
7. Lightly beat the remaining 2 eggs, dip the pieces into the egg and then into the breadcrumbs, and deep fry them in the oil until uniformly brown on all sides. Drain them on absorbent paper and serve hot, sprinkled with icing sugar.

Aranci caramellizzati
Caramelized Oranges

This recipe comes from Dodici Apostoli in Verona.

Serves 6

6 seedless oranges
1 cup (8 oz) sugar

1¼ cups (10 fl oz) water
1 tablespoon orange liqueur

1. With a very sharp knife, peel off the top layer of the orange skin and cut it into very fine strips.
2. Place the strips in a saucepan and add just enough water to cover. Simmer them for 5 to 6 minutes.
3. Peel the oranges carefully, removing all traces of white pith.
4. In a large saucepan combine the sugar and the water and simmer, stirring constantly, until the sugar has dissolved.
5. Boil the syrup for approximately 5 minutes, add the oranges and simmer for 2 to 3 minutes.
6. Remove the oranges and arrange them on a serving platter.
7. Place the strips of orange rind in the syrup and boil it gently until the syrup reaches the soft ball stage.
8. Cool the syrup slightly and add the orange liqueur.
9. Cool the syrup and pour it, together with the strips of rind, over the oranges.
10. Place them in the refrigerator and serve them chilled.

Index

A

Anchovies and tomatoes with spaghetti 60
Anchovy and garlic dip, Piemontese 128
Anchovy sauce with spaghetti 30
Artichoke omelette, Tuscan style 76
Artichokes, Calabrian style 33
Artichokes, Jewish style 12
Artichokes, stuffed 130
Artichokes, Venetian 142
Artichokes with kid 53
Asparagus and lettuce salad 130
Asparagus, Milanese style 102
Asparagus tips with spaghetti 68
Aubergine see Eggplant

Abbacchio al forno 97
Abbacchio alla cacciatora 10, 72
Abacchio arrosto 16
Agnello al fornello 52
Agnello alla cacciatora 65
Agnello con olive 96
Amarelli o amaretti di Modena 89
Anatra in salsa piccante 149
Anguilla in umido 148
Aranci caramellizzati 150
Arista alla genovese 125
Arrosto misto 46
Arselle alla maremmana 77
Asparagi alla milanese 102
Asticciola alla calabrese 37

B

Basil sauce, Ligurian 120
Beans and rice 96
Beans and tuna salad 36
Beans, broad, purée of 61
Bean soup, Tuscan 76
Béchamel sauce 104
Beef fillet, Sicilian style 44
Beef rolls, Calabrian stuffed 37
Beef stew, Genoese 122
Beef stew, Umbrian 70
Bolognese meat sauce 86
Bread soup 28
Broad beans, fresh, purée of 61
Broccoli, Milanese style 105
Broccoli with spaghetti 60

Baccalà alla vicentina 146
Baccalà mantecato 146
Bagna calda (or cauda) 126, 128
Bistecca alla fiorentina 80
Bistecca alla pizzaiola 25
Bollito misto 114
Broccoli o cavolfiori alla milanese 105
Brodetto alla anconetana 92
Bruschetta 66
Budino di cioccolata 117
Buttato 68

C

Calves' liver, Milanese 114
Calves' shank stew, Florentine style 81
Capsicums see Peppers
Cauliflower, fried, in batter 93
Cauliflower, Milanese style 105
Cauliflower salad 34
Cavatelli and turnips, Matera style 49
Celery, gratin of 104
Celery, roasted 48
Cheese and rice balls 141
Cheese and spinach pancakes 21
Cheese cake, Sicilian cream 45
Cheese dessert with rum, cream 117
Cheese fondue, Piedmontese 132
Chicken, Basilicata stuffed 50
Chicken consommé with passatelli 84
Chicken giblets and veal with polenta 141
Chicken liver croûtons with veal escalopes 70
Chicken marengo 133
Chicken, poached, with egg and lemon sauce 97
Chicken, Sicilian Sautéed 44
Chicken soup 136

Chicken, spit-roasted, with piquant rice 148
Chicken with meat sauce 78
Chicken with peppers 50
Chocolate cream, chilled, with lady fingers 116
Chocolate pudding 116
Christmas cake, Roman 17
Christmas cake, traditional, from Siena 81
Clam soup, Meapolitan 20
Clams, Sicilian steamed 42
Clams (mussels) with macaroni 29
Clams (pippies), Maremma style 77
Cod (stockfish) dried, with potatoes 94
Cod see also Salt cod
Consommé with dumplings 68
Cushions of Teramo 57
Custard pieces, Venetian deep fried 150
Cuttlefish, stuffed 62

Calamaretti delle Marche 96
Calzone 22
Canederli tirolesi 140
Caponata alla siciliana 38, 41
Cappon magro 118
Capretto e carciofi 53
Carciofi alla giudia 12
Carciofi alla veneziana 142
Carciofi gallico marina 33
Carciofi ripieni 130
Cassata alla siciliana 45
Cavatelli e rape alla materana 49
Cavolfiore fritto 93
Ciamotta 53
Cima alla genovese 118, 124
Cipolle ripiene alla piemontese 129
Cipolline in agrodolce 14
Coda alla vaccinara 16
Coniglio alla lucana 52
Costoletta di maiale alla napoletana 25
Costolette alla bolognese 87
Costolette alla milanese 110
Costolette di maiale 113
Costoletti di vitello con fontina (alla valdostana) 133
Cozze ripiene al sugo 64
Crema al mascarpone 117
Crema fritta all veneta 150
Crespolini al formaggio 21
Crocchetti di riso palermitana 40
Crostini di fegato 70
Cuscinetti di Teramo 57

D

Duck in piquant sauce 149
Dumplings, Tirolean 140
Dumplings with consommé 68

E

Eel casserole 148
Egg and lemon sauce with poached chicken 97
Egg noodles, Abruzzi 56
Eggplant, roasted 61
Eggplant, saute of 32
Eggplants, stuffed 33
Eggplant with cheese 41
Eggs, Florentine 77
Eggs, poached, with soup 101

F

Fennel with macaroni 48
Figs, stuffed 37
Fish chowder, Ancona 92
Fish soup, Capri 20
Fish steaks, Sicilian 42

Fave in bianco 61
Fegato alla veneziana 134, 149
Fegato di vitello alla milanese 114
Fichi ripieni 37
Filetti di baccalà 49
Filetti di tacchino 106
Filetto alla siciliana 44

Fonduta 126
Fonduta alla piemontese 132
Frittata con piselli 144
Fritto misto 24
Fritto misto alla fiorentina 80
Funghi ripieni alla piemontese 128

G

Garlic and anchovy dip, Piemontese 128
Garlic toast 66
Gorgonzola biscuits 116
Gratin of celery 104
Green sauce with mixed boiled meats 114

Gelato di fragole alla napoletana 25
Gniummerieddi 58
Gnocchi alla piemontese 132
Granita di limone 45, 73
Gremolata 110

I

Ice cream, Neapolitan strawberry 25

Insalata alla moda d'Alba 130
Insalata di cavolfiore 34
Insalata conti 36

K

Kebabs, mixed meat 72
Kid with artichokes 53

L

Lamb, Hunter's style 72
Lamb, roast baby 96
Lamb, roast, with potatoes 16
Lamb, spit-roasted 52
Lamb stew with tomatoes and potatoes 65
Lamb with olives 96
Lamb with risotto, Venetian 140
Lasagna, Calabrian 30
Lasagna, Ferrara style 84
Lasagna, rich 93
Lemon granita 73
Lemon water ice 45
Lettuce and asparagus salad 130
'Little Rags' 12
Liver, calves', Milanese 114
Liver, Venetian style 149

Lasagna alla calabrese 30
Lasagna all ferrarese 84
Lesso misto con salsa verde 114

M

Macaroni 13
Macaroni, Calabrian 29
Macaroni with clams or mussels 29
Macaroni with fennel 48
Meat balls or rissoles, Italian 113
Meat loaf, Italian 112
Meat sauce, Bolognese 86
Meat sauce with chicken 78
Meats, boiled, with green sauce 114
Mixed fry 24
Mixed fry in the Florentine manner 80
Mozzarella sandwich, toasted 56
Mullet, Calabrian 37
Mullet, red, Leghorn style 76
Mushroom and veal sauce 120
Mushrooms, Piedmontese stuffed 128
Mussels, stuffed, in tomato sauce 64
Mussels, Venetian style 145
Mussels see also Clams

Maccheroni alla calabrese 29
Maccheroni alla chitarra 56
Maccheroni con finocchio 48
Maccheroni con vongole o cozze 29
Melanzane al forno 61
Melanzane al funghetto 32
Melanzane alla siciliana 41
Melanzane ripiene 33
Minestra di passatelli 84

INDEX

Minestra di passatelli dell'Umbrio 68
Minestrone alla genovese 121
Minestrone alla milanese 100
Mozzarella in carrozza 56

O

Octopus, pickled 64
Onion pie 105
Onion soup 48
Onions, Piedmontese stuffed 129
Onions, sweet-and-sour 14
Oranges, caramelized 150
Oxtail, braised, shepherd style 16
Oysters, Venetian style 145

Ossobuco alla milanese 110
Ostriche alla veneziana 145

P

Pancakes, Abruzzi stuffed 57
Pancakes, cheese and spinach 21
Parmesan spinach 105
Parsley sauce, milanese 101
Pasta with sardines 40
Pea, green, omelette 144
Peas and rice, Venetian 136
Peppers, braised 144
Peppers, casserole of 34
Peppers, pickled 62
Peppers with chicken 50
Peverada sauce 148
Pimentos, Piemontese 129
Pine nut fondant 73
Pippies (clams), Maremma style 77
Pizza, Calabrian 28
Pizza, country-style 92
Pizza, Neapolitan 22
Pizza, turnover 22
Polenta with veal and chicken giblets 141
Pork chops, Neapolitan 25
Pork chops, with garlic and white wine 113
Pork, loin of, with garlic and rosemary 124
Potato cake, Trieste 142
Potato gnocchi 132

Pancotto 28
Panforte 81
Pangiallo alla romana 17
Papriche Veneziane 144
Pasta con le sarde alla palermitana 40
Pasta genovese 125
Pastella 24
Patate alla triestina 142
Peòci al pangrattato 145
Peperoni alla calabrese 34
Peperoni alla piemontese 129
Peperoni sott'aceto 62
Pesto 118, 120
Pinoccate di Perugia 73
Pizza alla napoletana 22
Pizza calabrese 28
Pizza rustica 92
Pizzette al Gorgonzola 116
Polenta 98, 101
Polenta pastizzada 141
Pollo alla diavola 78
Pollo alla maceratese 97
Pollo alla marengo 133
Pollo allo spiedo con riso in peverada 148
Pollo con peperoni 50
Pollo grillettato alla siciliana 44
Polloripieno alla lucana 50
Polpette 113
Polpettone 112
Polpi sott'aceto 64
Pomodori ripieni 69
Pomodori ripieni di cannolicchi 36

R

Rabbit in vinegar sauce 52
Ratatouille, Sicilian 41
Ravioli stuffed with fish and ricotta cheese 121
Rice and beans 96
Rice and cheese balls 141
Rice and peas, Venetian 136
Rice croquettes, Palermo 40
Rice, piquant, with spit-roasted chicken 148
Rice with veal sauce 122

Ricotta, fried 65
Risotto, black 137
Risotto, seafood 138
Risotto with beef marrow and white wine 102
Risotto with fish stock and wine 138
Risotto with lamb, Venetian 140
Risotto with zucchini 137

Ragù alla bolognese 86
Ravioli di magro 121
Ricotta fritta 65
Rigatoni 13
Risi e bisi 136
Riso alla genovese 122
Riso e fagioli 96
Risotto alla milanese 102
Risotto con le zucchete 137
Risotto di mare 138
Risotto di pesce a la ciosota 138
Risotto in capro roman 140
Risotto nero 137
Rotolo alla primavera 104

S

Salad of beans and tuna 36
Salt cod, cream of 146
Salt cod, fried fillets of 49
Salt cod, Vincenza 146
Sardines with pasta 40
Sauce diablo 78
Scaloppine in Marsala 108
Scaloppine in piquant sauce 108
Scaloppine Milanese style 108
Scaloppine with capers 108
Scaloppine with cheese 108
Scaloppine with olive oil and lemon 108
Scaloppine with tomatoes 108
Seafood risotto 138
Sole, steamed 65
Soup with poached eggs 101
Spaghetti 13
Spaghetti with anchovies and tomatoes 60
Spaghetti with anchovy sauce and breadcrumbs 30
Spaghetti with asparagus tips 68
Spaghetti with broccoli 60
Spaghetti with squid or cuttlefish 60
Spaghetti with tomato and vegetable sauce 32
Spaghetti with tomatoes, cheese and bacon 24
Spinach and cheese pancakes 21
Spinach, Parmesan 105
Spinach with pine nuts and raisins 122
Sponge cake, Genoese 125
Spring roll 104
Squid in wine and chilli sauce 96
Squid (or cuttlefish) with spaghetti 60
Steak, Florentine style 80
Steak, Neapolitan 25
Strawberry ice cream, Neapolitan 25

Salsa alla diavola 78
Salsa genovese 120
Salsa verde 114
Salsa verde alla milanese 101
Saltimbocca alla rimana 17
Scaloppe farcite 112
Scaloppine al fromaggio 108
Scaloppine alla milanese 108
Scaloppine alla perugina 70
Scaloppine al Marsala 108
Scaloppine al pomodore 108
Scaloppine con i capperi 108
Scaloppine con olio e lemone 108
Scaloppine in salsa picanta 108
Scampi alla veneziana 134
Scrippelle 'mbusse 57
Sedano al forno 48
Sedano alla milanese 104
Semifreddo di cioccolata 116
Seppie ripiene 62
Soffrito 68
Sogiole al piatto 65
Spaghetti a cacio e pepe 13
Spaghetti alla carbonara 13
Spaghetti alla napoletana 24
Spaghetti alla prestinara 15
Spaghetti alla sangiovanniello 60
Spaghetti al sugo 32

Spaghetti ammollicato 30
Spaghetti con i broccoli 60
Spaghetti con le seppie 60
Spaghetti con punte d'asparagi 68
Spezzato di tacchino 69
Spiedini misti spoletani 72
Spinaci alla liguria 122
Spinaci alla parmigiana 105
Stoccafisso all'anconitana 94
Stracciatella 12
Stufatino umbrese 70
Stufato di manzo alla genovese 122
Suppli al telefono 141

T

Tomato and vegetable sauce with spaghetti 32
Tomatoes and anchovies with spaghetti 60
Tomatoes, stuffed 69
Tomatoes stuffed with cannolicchi pasta 36
Tortellini, Bolognese style 85
Tripe, Roman style 14
Tripe soup 100
Tuna mayonnaise 109
Tune with olives and capers 42
Turkey, breasts of 106
Turkey, Lombardian stuffed 106
Turkey, Umbrian casserole of, with olives 69
Turnips and cavatelli, Matera style 49

Tacchina ripiena alla lombarda 106
Tonno alla marinara 42
Torta di carciofi alla toscana 76
Torta di cipolle 105
Tortellini bolognese 85
Trance di pesce alla siciliana 42
Triglie alla calabrese 37
Triglie alla livornese 76
Trippa alla romana 14

U

Uova alla fiorentina 77

V

Veal and chicken giblets with polenta 141
Veal and mushroom sauce 120
Veal chops with Fontina cheese 133
Veal, cold braised, with tuna mayonnaise 109
Veal cutlets, Bolognese style 86
Veal cutlets, Milanese 110
Veal escalopes, Genoese style 124
Veal escalopes, stuffed 112
Veal escalopes with chicken liver croûtons, Perugina style 70
Veal sauce with rice 122
Veal shanks, Milan style 110
Veal, small escalopes of, Milanese style 108
Veal, stuffed shoulder or breast 124
Veal with ham and sage 17
Vegetables, deep fried 53
Vegetable soup, Genoese 121
Vegetable soup, Milanese thick 100
Vinegar sauce, rabbit in 52

Vincisgrassi 90, 93
Vitello alla genovese 124
Vitello tonnato 109
Vongole alla siciliana 42

W

Wine and chilli sauce, squid in 96

Z

Zucchini, marinated 62
Zucchini with risotto 137

Zabaione 44
Zampa alla fiorentina 81
Zucchini in marinata 62
Zuppa di cipolle 48
Zuppa di fagioli alla toscana 76
Zuppa di pesce caprese 20
Zuppa di pollo 136
Zuppa di trippa 100
Zuppa di vongole 20
Zuppa pavese 101